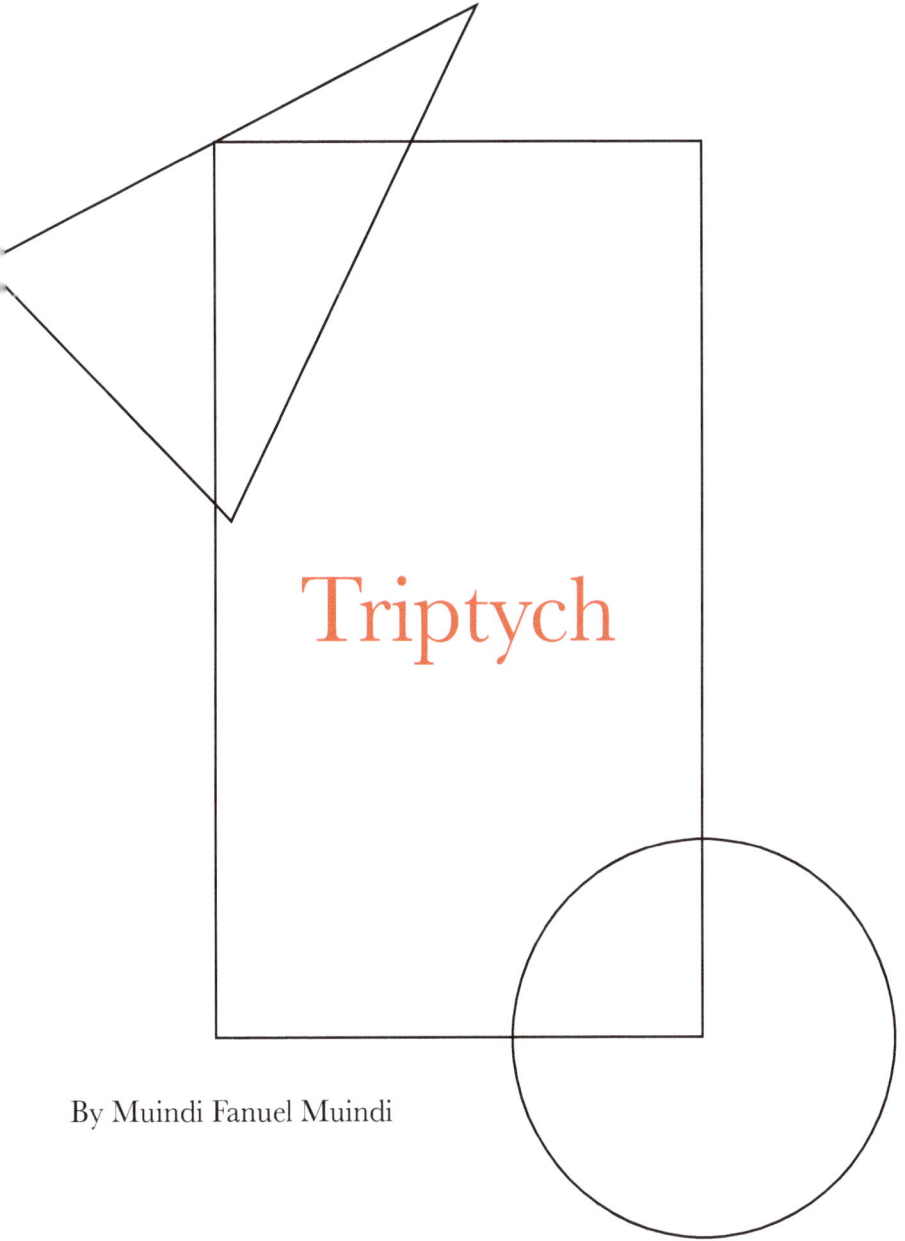

Triptych

By Muindi Fanuel Muindi

SFPML

SFPML

www.solutionsforpostmodernliving.com

First Printing, 2019

Copyright © 2019 by Muindi Fanuel Muindi

Designed by Muindi Fanuel Muindi

ISBN 978-0-578-56410-4

for ylfa

CONTENTS

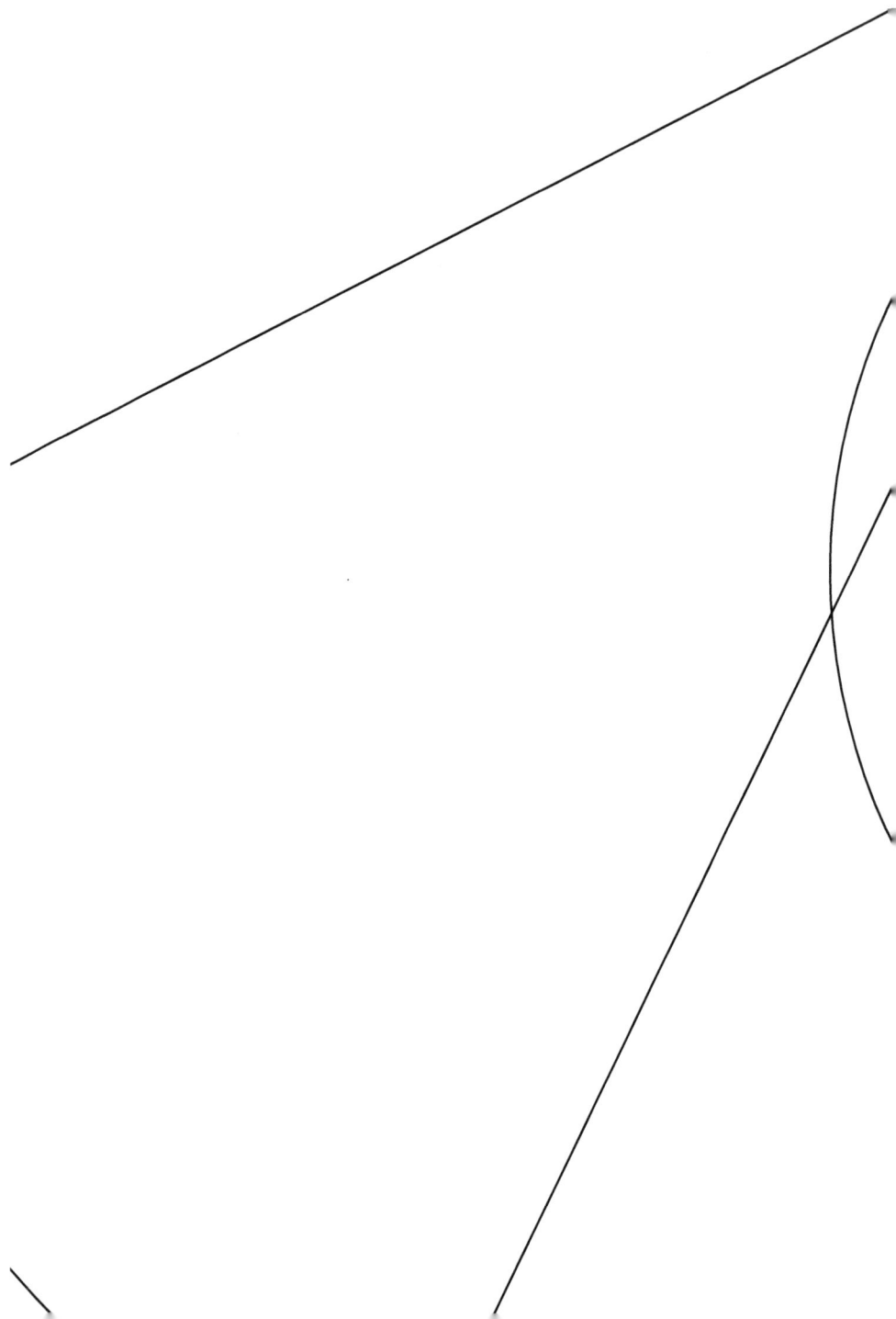

"It is well known that the total book is as much Leibniz's dream as Mallarmé's, even though they never stop working in fragments. Our error is in believing that they did not succeed in their wishes: they make this unique book perfectly, the book of monads, in letters and little circumstantial pieces that could sustain as many dispersions as combinations."

Gilles Deleuze, *The Fold*

"… the important thing above all is not to understand, the important thing is to take on the rhythm of a given man, a given writer, a given philosopher…"

Gilles Deleuze, Cours Vincennes à Saint-Denis: 'On Kant', 1978

Whither,

Otherwise

3

No nation, race nor tribe, no bonds of common kind,
No assignation shared, no custom yet contrived
Nor e'er to come, no place, in spite
Of birth, do I esteem.
Belonging? Fie! To cultivate
A will to deviate,

Examine and explode! Aye! A will to deviate,
Except myself from kith and kind—
To dare! To cultivate
A sense and discourse bold, contrived,
Remorseless, strange! Esteem,
Authority, returns: when means conforming, spite;

When means transforming, joy! In spite
Of cast, to deviate—
No lot endure in peace lest I succumb. Esteem,
Authority, returns employ as means to cut unkind,
Lethargic, timid chaff. Contrive
As foe who'd cultivate

A norm, as friend who'd cultivate
Anomalies. To spite
The glut of common goods—expenditures contrived
As rare, auratic works commission! Deviate!
Announce myself uncommon kind,
Exceptional! Esteem

From vicious circles woo; from virtue's thralls, esteem
Eschew for rancor. Cultivate
An oddity, the kind
Of monster righteous foils would spite:
A creature deviate,
A villain challenging, a menace queer. Contrive

To grasp this horror's truth. Contrive
To win this fiend's esteem.
Conspire together, deviates:
Ally to cultivate
Yet more exceptions brave who agitate and spite
The vulgar. Misanthrope am I? A wretched kind?

—For I contrive to cultivate
A soul's esteem or spite
As spur to deviate from common kind.

Daemonic Ecologues: I - IV

I.

> Forested: niches
> plenty, chorus dissonant.
> Call it madness?

II.

> Mannerly, yielding—
> fields of grain as far as the
> eye can see—a yawn.

III.

> Spectators, many,
> heeded; beasts, untamable,
> trapped, menageried.

IV.

> Bristlecones—weathered,
> twisted, ancients! Wonder at
> time's asymmetry!

V.

    Mental disorders
    cataloged; flock ravagers
    tagged for culling.

VI.

    Noumena: vampire
    squids from Hell—the quarry of
    giant grenadiers.

VII.

    Things-in-themselves: grim
    alpine raptors scavenging,
    spurning meat for bone.

VIII.

    Inwardness thaws; blooms
    action, passion! Tundra in
    hues resplendent!

Daemonic Ecologues: IX - XII

IX.

Trial by fire
sought for, craved. Shoots burgeoning.
Blessed, charred soils!

X.

Feraled domestics,
pigeons, rats—the demagogue's
quirks and foibles nag.

XI.

Carnage! Hyaenas
bicker, jostle—ravenous.
Feast on my darlings!

XII.

Trauma transforms us—
mass extinction, stimulus—
species radiate.

I. Proem

Sufficiency, disdain'd—of surfeit, fond;
Excrescences of culture, decadence,
   Like cocksure pheasants' feathers, proudly donn'd.
Sufficiency, disdain'd—of surfeit, fond;
From foul, excess outgrowths, beauty dawn'd—
   Came plumage, warbles, wattles—exquisite!
Sufficiency, disdain'd—of surfeit, fond.
Through excrescence of culture, decadence,
   The necessary, mock'd—with not, fared more.
   When life, from seas, surfac'd, wriggl'd ashore,
     Excrescences found purposes profound:
     Moisture retain'd, 'came limbs that trod the ground.
      "Were not all creatures un-submerg'd done for?"
     The necessary, mock'd—with not, fared more!

II. To Samuel Beckett

The necessary, mock'd—with not, fair'd more:
No plot, no characters, no setting fix'd—
   And yet the heartstrings pull'd, the affects sure!
The necessary, mock'd—with not, fair'd more:
Just larval subjects, objects *sous rature*,
   A narrative as tangible as mist.
The necessary, mock'd—with not, fair'd more.
No plot, no characters, no setting fix'd,
   No in-betweens: aboves, belows, beyonds—
   Digressive to no end, no denouement.
    With strange attractors, fractal dynamics,
     Keen patterned chaos, yet dealt less pricks than kicks.
     Nohow on, the fizzles correspond!
     No in-betweens: aboves, belows, beyonds!

Paeans: III & IV

III. To Friedrich Nietzsche (for Jon)

No in-betweens: aboves, belows, beyonds!
The will to power, sickness unto life—
   A pregnancy from which a mutant spawn'd.
No in-betweens: aboves, belows, beyonds!
The overman: forebear *and* prodigal son—
   Ne'er yet the species next; 'strang'd prototype.
No in-betweens: aboves, belows, beyonds!
The will to power, sickness unto life—
   Sufficiency, disdain'd—of surfeit, fond.
   Untimely ones, no lineage hing'd upon—
     Living proof of danger's immanence;
     Against their thriving, all establishments.
       Firstlings *and* endlings, thus, their *sine qua non*—
       Sufficiency, disdain'd—of surfeit, fond.

IV. To James Joyce

Sufficiency, disdain'd—of surfeit, fond:
A fugue of plots and puns clanging a round—
   A sounding follow up to Moll's run-ons.
Sufficiency, disdain'd—of surfeit, fond;
A hypertrophied, florid lexicon—
   Babbling abundance, dialects confound.
Sufficiency, disdain'd—of surfeit, fond;
A fugue of plots and puns clanging a round.
The necessary, mock'd—from fate, abscond!
   Harold, Anna, Issy, Shem and Shaun—
     The scandals that embroil'd them unteas'd
     From Anna's gramme—such plurabilities—
       Sign'd each a counterplotted pantheon.
       The necessary, mock'd—from fate, abscond!

V. To Emily Brontë (for ylfa)

The necessary, mock'd—from fate, abscond!
What joys belied by spleen from Nelly Dean!
  She ne'er spoke straight of sins she'd have forgone.
The necessary, mock'd—from fate, abscond!
Beneath the downy heaths they moan anon—
  Ruder, stranger productions, scenes obscene.
The necessary, mock'd—from fate, abscond!
What joys belied by spleen from Nelly Dean!
  Becomings, definite; beings, obscur'd!
  An abject love—intensity assured!
    Cathy bewill'd 'midst Heath—within, without,
    With him whither, *this* Other, for, no doubt,
      Upon the Craggs, above the Heights, recurr'd—
      Becomings, definite; beings, obscur'd.

VI. To Anaïs Nin

Becomings, definite; beings, obscur'd;
Her days plotted—untold trajectories,
  Accretions, evolutions, en-contours.
Becomings, definite; beings, obscur'd;
Her diaries, a foam of *mémoires pure*,
  Of base matter and lived intensities.
Becomings, definite; beings, obscur'd;
Her days plotted—untold trajectories—
  Sufficiency, disdain'd—of surfeit, fond.
  Regard, her phase portraits of liaisons,
    Interior crises, blue sky catastrophes,
    Attractors merg'd and Eros, dystheity
      Of seduction, englamour'd, champion'd!
      Sufficiency, disdain'd—of surfeit, fond.

VII. To Georges Bataille

Sufficiency disdain'd—of surfeit, fond;
Economiz'd—revel'd in luxury!
  Austerity, for shame, an excess unreckon'd!
Sufficiency disdain'd—of surfeit, fond;
While sov'reigns hail the sumptuous, thralls and bonds
  Err, pit utility 'gainst penury.
Sufficiency disdain'd—of surfeit, fond;
Economiz'd—revel'd in luxury!
  The necessary mock'd—with not, fared more!
  A riddle for those who champion the poor,
    Play foils to rakes, and fetishize basic needs:
    Your justice would profligacy impede?
      With Maxwell's demon have you curried favor?
      The necessary mock'd—with not, fared more!

VIII. To Thelonious Monk

The necessary, mock'd—with not, fair'd more.
Bad chops—with baffling, flat, rattling attacks,
  Notes crush'd and wraith'd at varying odds—the bettor!
The necessary mocked—with not, fair'd more;
Chance discords return'd, then underscor'd, then call'd for—
  "A Jabberwocky'd jazz?" His ditties wisecrack'd.
The necessary, mocked—with not, fair'd more.
Bad chops—with baffling, flat, rattling attacks,
  Join'd minimal and maximal extremes,
  Contingencies composed into his themes
    Do traces of embodiment lay bare—
    Turns kinesthetic and melodic cohere.
      A neighbor glanc'd and horses chang'd midstream!
      Join'd minimal and maximal extremes.

IX. To Marcel Duchamp

Join'd minimal and maximal extremes:
Creator 'gainst spectator—queer kind of chess.
   Check—*mise en scène!* And mate—*mise en abyme!*
Join'd minimal and maximal extremes:
The art—the fossils kept safe in museums;
   The life of the artist—the danger in the flesh.
Join'd minimal and maximal extremes:
Creator 'gainst spectator—queer kind of chess.
   No rudiments, but supplements supreme—
    To wit: a counter-signifying regime,
      Networks of stoppages that free the play of signs.
      Is not this game De Quincey's perfect crime—
        The murder of the real? Devious, his scheme:
        No rudiments, but supplements supreme.

X. To Jean Dubuffet

No rudiments, but supplements supreme!
Assembl'd leftovers—sundry odds and ends
   Forag'd, scaveng'd, their usage unforeseen.
No rudiments, but supplements supreme!
Culture's offal through bricolage beseem'd
   With natures excrements, cursed dividends.
No rudiments, but supplements supreme!
Assembl'd leftovers—sundry odds and ends,
   Interiors formless, boundaries baroque,
   Objects impervious to common tropes,
    Affinity and enmity set free,
      And rife 'tempts at decipherment stymied.
        Art brut, a private language approach'd—
        Interiors formless, boundaries baroque.

Paeans: XI & XII

XI. To Maya Deren (for Cáit)

Interiors formless, boundaries baroque—
Discern'd not time as 'twas, but time as 'twas not—
  Grasp'd time as it becomes, from space unyok'd.
Interiors formless, boundaries baroque—
When graph'd—shots, tangent curves; cuts, asymptotes;
  Each montage, an infinity traversed in thought.
Interiors formless, boundaries baroque—
Discern'd not time as 'twas, but time as 'twas not,
  Black stars and singularities, invok'd—
    The regions, objects, space-times which connote
      Durations, rituals. Miscalculations
    Of origins expos'd in cogitations,
        Obsessions, compulsions—forlorn hopes.
        Black stars and singularities, invok'd.

XII. To J. Robert Oppenheimer

Black stars and singularities, invok'd.
Probed nature like a gnostic thaumaturge—
  Enigmas, his untimely masterstrokes.
Black stars and singularities, invok'd.
The Desert Fathers of Big Science, convok'd,
  Batter'd the heart or matter—the Gadget, a scourge!
Black stars and singularities, invok'd.
Probed nature like a gnostic thaumaturge—
  The universe implod'd at its seams,
  The impermeable became a porous screen,
      Came Death to the World, and all our woe—
      Archontes and Demiurge triumphant, aglow!
    At Trinity, Heimarmene redeem'd—
      The universe implod'd at its seams.

13

XIII. To Gertrude Stein

The universe implod'd at its seems—
For she suppos'd that grammar 'ploy'd invention,
  Came conjugation 'fore declension—verbs teem'd.
The universe, implod'd, as it seems,
Explod'd, as it means, transplod'd, meme'd—
  Gush'd floating signifiers; referents, punn'd.
The universe, implod'd, at its seems—
For she suppos'd that grammar 'ploy'd invention,
  Join'd minimal and maximal extremes,
   The slightest differences, the unforeseen,
   Found she, repeating things insistently.
   She then insist'd things incessantly,
     And incessant difference in insistence glean'd,
     Join'd minimal and maximal extremes.

XIV. To the Marquis de Sade

Join'd minimal and maximal extremes:
Not faith in reason—an acute passion for it!
  The boudoir o'er the towers of academe,
Join'd minimal and maximal extremes.
Freethinking—eroticiz'd by libertines—
  When institutionaliz'd 'came impotent.
Join'd minimal and maximal extremes:
Not faith in reason—an acute passion for it!
  Sufficiency, disdain'd—of surfeit, fond;
  With morals there could be no rapprochement.
   Hailed apathy—virulent, pernicious, cruel—
   For he saw in this affliction reason's fuel,
     And reason enjoy'd to excess *au fond*.
     Sufficiency, disdain'd—of surfeit, fond.

XV. Recapitulation

Sufficiency, disdain'd—of surfeit, fond;
The necessary, mock'd—with not, fare'd more.
 No in-betweens: aboves, belows, beyonds!
Sufficiency, disdain'd—of surfeit, fond;
The necessary, mock'd—from fate, abscond!
 Becomings, definite; beings, obscur'd.
Sufficiency, disdain'd—of surfeit, fond.
The necessary, mock'd—with not, fair'd more:
 Join'd minimal and maximal extremes,
  No rudiments, but supplements supreme,
   Interiors formless, boundaries baroque,
   Black stars and singularities, invok'd
    The universe implod'd at its seams,
    Join'd minimal and maximal extremes.

I.

Toast the pyrrhic triumph of reason, proud fiends!
For afore our fetish for reason marked us,
Wanton fantasts driven to doubt. — *Out, damned spot,*
Craving to query!

For afore our fetish for reason marked us;
Now, my weyward foulers, behold! Though wanting
Cravings to query,
Bores yet feign a ratiocinative stance!

Yes! My weyward foulers, behold! Though wanting
Our cruel conscience, genius for skepticism,
Boors yet feign a ratiocinative stance!
Threatened, they bristle—

Our cruel conscience, genius for skepticism,
Simulated crudely to ward off danger.
Threatened, they bristle;
Constant danger, constant their bristling.

II.

Instrumental reason? An affectation!
Matters of fact? Fine
Subterfuges, means to avert predation—

Some rough beast, some monstrous aberration
Sighted in outline!
Instrumental reason? An affectation!

Our keen questions, poisonous cogitations
Mimicked—burlesque signs,
Subterfuges, means to avert predation!

Progress trap—great maw of that sphinx, Stagnation—
Cavernous, sighing.
Instrumental reason? An affectation!

Dazed Stagnation, fearing transvaluation,
Shrinks at their droll mimes,
Subterfuges, means to avert predation.

Sphinx! Loathe host vessel for our transformations!
Shrug their disguise! Dine!
Instrumental reason? An affectation,
Subterfuge—a means to avert predation!

III.

Riddles borne—our larval and pupal stages—
Virulent phages!

Riddles passed—our winged imagos molt free—
Dipterous lovelies!

She withstands our parasitism sorely—
Costlies, such glories!

Cruel sphinx, cursed to find us amongst your quarry —
Toast to you who bears us in rank excrescence!
Gorged, recline in languorous convalescence!
Virulent phages! Dipterous lovelies! Costlies, such glories!

Lexicon for a Language Game:

1.1: A **trace** is a sense impression.

1.2: A **process** is the production of a trace.

1.2.1: **Regularizing processes**, a.k.a., *synchronous* processes, are processes that produce *regular* traces, a.k.a., phenomenal presences.

1.2.1.1: A **phenomenal presence** is a sense impression of a being, a *fact* of spacing and temporizing. A phenomenal presence indexes the manner and extent to which one has acted.

1.2.1.1.1: A **phenomenal presence of action** is an index of the manner and extent to which one has actively acted—e.g., the manner and extent to which one has seen.

1.2.1.1.1.1: The phenomenal presence of one's actions is always concomitantly the phenomenal presence of others' passions—e.g., an index of the manner and extent to which one has seen is always concomitantly an index of the manner and extent to which others have made themselves seen.

1.2.1.1.2: A **phenomenal presence of reflection** is an index of the manner and extent to which one has reflexively acted—e.g., the manner and extent to which one has seen oneself.

1.2.1.1.3: A **phenomenal presence of passion** is an index of the manner and extent to which one has passively acted—e.g., the manner and extent to which one has made oneself seen by others.

1.2.1.1.3.1: The phenomenal presence of one's passions is always concomitantly the phenomenal presence of others' actions—e.g., an index of the manner and extent to which one has made oneself seen is always concomitantly an index of the manner and extent to which others have seen.

1.2.2: **Singularizing processes**, a.k.a., *asynchronous* processes, are processes that produce *singular* traces, a.k.a., enigmatic absences.

1.2.2.1: An **enigmatic absence** is a sense impression of a becoming, an *act* of spacing and temporizing. An enigmatic absence indexes one's power to act.

1.2.2.1.1: An **enigmatic absence of action** is an index of one's power to actively act—e.g., one's power to see.

1.2.2.1.1.1: The enigmatic absence of one's actions is always concomitantly the enigmatic absence of others' passions—e.g. an index of one's power to see is always concomitantly an index of another's power to make themself seen.

1.2.2.1.2: An *enigmatic absence of reflection* is an index one's power to reflexively act—e.g., one's power to see oneself.

1.2.2.1.3: An *enigmatic absence of passion* is an index of ones power to passively act—e.g., one's power to make oneself seen by others.

1.2.2.1.3.1: The enigmatic absence of one's passions is always concomitantly the enigmatic absence of others' actions—e.g. an index of one's power to make oneself seen is always an index of another's power to see.

1.3: To *act* is to access a process; to *access a process* is to affect the production of a trace.

1.3.1: To access to a regularizing process is to direct the production of a phenomenal presence or, in other words, to *regulate* the manner and extent to which one has acted.

1.3.1.1: A *regular action* regulates the manner and extent to which one has actively acted and, concomitantly, the manner and extent to which others have passively acted.

1.3.1.2: A *regular reflection* regulates the manner and extent to which one has reflexively acted.

1.3.1.3: A *regular passion* regulates the manner and extent to which one has passively acted and, concomitantly, the manner and extent to which others have actively acted.

1.3.2: To access a singularizing process is to affect the production of an enigmatic absence or, in other words, to *probe* ones power to act.

1.3.2.1: A *singular action* probes one's own power to actively act and, concomitantly, others' powers to passively act.

1.3.2.2: A *singular reflection* probes one's own power to reflexively act.

1.3.2.3: A *singular passion* probes one's own power to passively act and, concomitantly, others' powers to actively act.

2.1: A process is ***accessed intuitively*** or ***sensed*** when one generates and/or interprets sensory signs of a process.

2.1.1: The ***sensory signs*** of a process are the following: traces, situations, desires, fluxes and impulses.

2.1.1.1: ***Traces*** are sense impressions produced by processes.

2.1.1.1.1: A ***phenomenal presence*** is a trace produced by regularizing processes.

2.1.1.1.2: An ***enigmatic absence*** is a trace produced by singularizing processes.

2.1.1.2: ***Situations*** are gestalts in which traces of different processes are presented together as integrated parts of a consistent whole which affords one or more actions, passions, or reflections.

2.1.1.2.1: Situations are ***composite to infinity***. One situation may itself contain other situations, which may themselves contain other situations, which may themselves contain other situations, which may themselves contain other situations, on to infinity.

2.1.1.2.2: An ***affordance*** is a potential for action, reflection, or passion developed via a situation.

2.1.1.2.2.1: A situation is ***singularizing*** to the degree that it affords singular actions, refections, and passions

2.1.1.2.2.2: A situation is ***regularizing*** to the degree that it affords regular actions, reflections, and passions.

2.1.1.2.3: ***Consistency*** is the condition of cohering, holding together, and retaining form. A situation that is not consistent is no situation at all—a situation coheres, holds together, and retains its form in spite of influxes and outfluxes of traces.

2.1.1.2.3.1: Individuals cannot simply situate traces as they are—individuals distort traces in order to make them cohere.

2.1.1.2.3.1.1: The ***manifest contents*** of a situation are those aspects of traces that are included in a situation following distortions; the manifest contents form the ***figure*** of a situation.

2.1.1.2.3.1.2: The ***latent contents*** of a situation are the aspects of traces that are excluded from a situation via distortion only to form a situation's bounds or limits, the border between what is outside a given situation and what is inside, a region where consistency verges on inconsistency and vice versa. In other words, the latent contents form the ***ground*** of a situation.

2.1.1.2.3.1.3: The phenomenal presences of actions, reflections, and passions are always inconsistent with corresponding enigmatic absences of actions, reflections, and passions, and vice versa—e.g., the phenomenal presences that index the manner and extent to which one has seen are inconsistent with the enigmatic absences that index one's power to see.

2.1.1.2.3.1.3.1: The degree to which a given situation is more singularizing than regularizing is the degree to which enigmatic absences are more manifest than their corresponding phenomenal presences in the given situation, and vice versa.

2.1.1.3: **Desires** are motives which affect situations of traces.

2.1.1.3.1: A **desire to express an impression** affects the situation of a trace to the degree that a trace is manifest in a situation.

2.1.1.3.2: A **desire to repress an impression** affects the situation of a trace to the degree that a trace is latent in a situation.

2.1.1.4: **Fluxes**, or **fluctuations of desire**, are movements of traces into and out of situations.

2.1.1.5: **Impulses** are motives which effect fluxes of traces.

2.1.1.5.1: A flux is effected by an **impulse to enjoy a repressed impression** to the degree that the latent becomes manifest following a flux. A flux is effected by an **impulse to repulse a repressed impression** to the degree that the latent remains latent following a flux.

2.1.1.5.2: A flux is effected by an **impulse to repulse an expressed impression** to the degree that the manifest becomes latent following a flux. A flux is effected by an **impulse to enjoy an expressed impression** to the degree that the manifest remains manifest following a flux.

2.1.1.5.3: A flux is effected by an **impulse to enjoy an undesired impression** to the degree that a previously un-situated trace becomes manifest following a flux. A flux is effected by an **impulse to repulse an undesired impression** to the degree that a previously un-situated trace becomes latent following a flux.

2.2: A process is **accessed rationally** or **understood** when one generates and/or interprets discursive signs and proto-discursive sensory signs of a process.

2.2.1: The **proto-discursive sensory signs** of a process are the sensory signs upon which discursive signs site affordances: situations and traces.

2.2.2: The **discursive signs** of a process are as follows: frames of reference, types, symbols, statements, enunciations, rules of inference, and arguments.

2.2.2.1: **Frames of reference** are indexical conventions which enable us to site affordances within and amongst situations and traces.

2.2.2.2: **Types** are categories of affordances that are abstracted from and either constatively re-sembled or performatively dis-sembled by traces that have been framed as sites of affordances.

2.2.2.2.1: **Exceptional types** are categories that only include singular affordances.

2.2.2.2.2: **Regular types** are categories that only include regular affordances.

2.2.2.2.3: **Ambivalent types** are categories that include both regular and singular affordances.

2.2.2.3: **Symbols** are traces framed as sites of affordances and, subsequently, cast as either constative re-semblings or performative dis-semblings of types.

2.2.2.3.1: **Singular symbols** are enigmatic absences sited as performative dis-semblings of ambivalent and exceptional types.

2.2.2.3.2: **Regular symbols** are phenomenal presences sited as constative re-semblings of ambivalent and regular types.

2.2.2.4: **Statements** are relationships between frames of reference, types, and symbols that are abstracted from and either performatively dis-sembled or constatively re-sembled by situations.

2.2.2.4.1: Relationships between frames of reference, types, and symbols are **apparent** when statements site affordances in a single situation or in situations that are parts of a single composite situation.

2.2.2.4.1.1: A statement of an apparent relationship is an **observation**.

2.2.2.4.1.1.1: Two different individuals demonstrate a shared **sensibility** when they make observations that are analogous or homologous.

2.2.2.4.2: Relationships between frames of reference, types, and symbols are **inferred** when statements site affordances in multiple situations that are not parts of a single composite situation.

2.2.2.4.2.1: A statement of an inferred relationship is an **inference**.

2.2.2.4.2.1.1: Two individuals demonstrate a **shared understanding** when they make inferences that are analogous or homologous.

2.2.2.5: **Enunciations** are situations sited as constative re-semblings and/or performative dis-semblings of statements.

2.2.2.5.1: An enunciation is a **performative dis-sembling** of a statement to the degree that an enunciation is a singularizing situation.

2.2.2.5.1: An enunciation is a **constative re-sembling** of a statement to the degree that an enunciation is a regularizing situation.

2.2.2.6: **Rules of inference** are generalized rules for relating frames of reference, situations, and symbols that are abstracted from particular statements and their enunciations.

2.2.2.6.1: **Inductive rules of inference** allow us to draw inferences on the basis of analogies and homologies between symbols.

2.2.2.6.2: **Deductive rules of inference** allow us to draw inferences on the basis of analogies and homologies between types.

2.2.2.6.3: **Abductive rules of inference** allow us to draw inferences on the basis of analogies and homologies between frames of reference.

2.2.2.7: **Arguments** are groups of statements sited as constative re-semblings of rules of inference.

2.3: An ***object*** is an assemblage of traces prefigured by a situation.

2.3.1: Traces are ***prefigured*** by a situation to the degree that they are ***virtually situated***—that is, to the degree that there are sites framed within a situation that anticipate the traces. A trace is not ***actually situated*** until an impulse drives a flux that incorporates a trace into a site within a situation.

2.3.2: Objects ***catalyze*** the impulses that drive the fluxes that would situate them.

2.3.3: ***Singularizing objects*** are prefigured by singularizing situations.

2.3.3.1: As each singularizing object facilitates probes, we call such objects ***probes*** and the impulses they catalyze ***impulses to probe***.

2.3.4: ***Regularizing objects*** are prefigured by regularizing situations.

2.3.4.1: As each regularizing object facilitates regulations, we may call such objects ***regulators*** and the impulses they catalyze ***impulses to regulate***.

2.4. A trace that is not prefigured by a situation is a ***partial object***.

2.5: A statement is a **known known** to the degree that the situations that enunciate the statement are concrete.

2.5.1: A situation is **concrete** to the degree that sites framed within a situation are occupied by traces via influxes of objects.

2.5.2: An enunciation of a known known is a product of **instrumental reasoning** to the degree that it is a constative re-sembling of a statement, and it is a product of **superfluous reasoning** to the degree that it is a performative dis-sembling of a statement.

2.6: A statement is an **known unknown** to the degree that the situations that enunciate the statement are abstract.

2.6.1: A situation is **abstract** to the degree sites framed within it are unoccupied by traces as a result of no fluxes or vacated by traces via outfluxes of objects.

2.6.1.1: An abstract situation is a product of **figmenting imagination** to the extent that it is a regularizing situation, and it is a product of **fragmenting imagination** to the extent that it is a singularizing situation.

2.7: **Unknown knowns** are abstract situations that have yet to be explicated—that is, abstract situations that have yet to be sited as enunciations of statements.

2.8: **Unknown unknowns** are partial objects.

2.9: **Unconscious imagination** establishes unknown knowns by situating unknown unknowns.

2.10: **Conscious imagination** establishes known unknowns by drawing inferences from known knowns.

2.11: **Interpretive reasoning** establishes known knowns by explicating unknown knowns.

2.12: **Investigative reasoning** establishes known knowns by evincing known unknowns.

2.13: **Recollective reasoning** re-enunciates known knowns.

3.1: *Identifications* are (i) actions through which one comes to associate others with types, or (ii) reflections through which one comes to associate oneself with a type, or (iii) passions through which others comes to associate one with a type.

3.1.1: One has an *exceptional identity* when one is identified with an singular symbol, whether by oneself or by others.

3.1.2: One has a *regular identity* when one is identified with a regular symbol, whether by oneself or by others.

3.2: One's *subjectivity* is determined by whether or not one enjoys or repulses the traces sited as symbols of their identity.

3.2.1: One has a *balanced subjectivity* to the degree that one enjoys one's regular identity—i.e., to the degree that one enjoys the phenomenal presences sited as symbols of one's regular identity.

3.2.2: One has a *hysterical subjectivity* to the degree that one repulses one's regular identity— i.e., to the degree that one repulses the phenomenal presences sited as symbols of one's regular identity.

3.2.3: One has a *perverse subjectivity* to the degree that one enjoys one's exceptional identity— i.e., to the degree that one enjoys the enigmatic absences sited as symbols of one's exceptional identity.

3.2.4: One has an *obsessional subjectivity* to the degree that one repulses one's exceptional identity— i.e., to the degree that one repulses the enigmatic absences sited as symbols of one's exceptional identity.

3.2: *Cultural apparatuses* are regulators that virtually afford regular identifications and either balanced or obsessive subjectivizations.

3.2.1: *Discursive cultural apparatuses* virtually afford regular identifications; *aesthetic cultural apparatuses* virtually afford balanced or obsessive subjectivizations.

3.3: *Countercultural apparatuses* are probes that virtually afford exceptional identifications and either hysterical or perverse subjectivizations.

3.3.1: *Discursive countercultural apparatuses* virtually afford exceptional identification; *aesthetic countercultural apparatuses* virtually afford hysterical or perverse subjectivizations.

3. Ethics

3.4: Situating a cultural apparatus facilitates **compliance with regulations** and situating a countercultural apparatus facilitates **breaches of regulations**; countercultural apparatuses are always superposed upon cultural apparatuses so as to produce interferences that override the affordances of cultural apparatuses.

3.5: To **conform** is to situate a cultural apparatus and comply with regulations.

3.5.1: **Conformers** are individuals who conform.

3.6: To **reform** is to develop cultural apparatuses that advance regulations.

3.6.1: **Reformers** are individuals who reform.

3.6.1.1: The **icon** is a reformer who develops aesthetic cultural apparatuses.

3.6.1.2: The **ideologue** is a reformer who develops discursive cultural apparatuses.

3.6.1.3: The **phenom** is a reformer who develops aesthetic cultural apparatuses *and* discursive cultural apparatuses.

3.7: To **deform** is to situate a counter-cultural apparatus and breach regulations.

3.7.1: **Deformers** are individuals who deform.

3.8: To **transform** is to develop countercultural apparatuses that advance breaches

3.8.1: **Transformers** are individuals who transform.

3.8.1.1: The **iconoclast** is a transformer who develops aesthetic countercultural apparatuses.

3.8.1.2: The **freethinker** is a transformer who develops discursive countercultural apparatuses.

3.8.1.3: The **enigma** is a transformer who develops aesthetic countercultural apparatuses *and* discursive countercultural apparatuses.

Hell is other people. — For to live amongst others is to be judged and found wanting. For how could I be represented otherwise than a wanting, a lacking, a nothing? To be represented otherwise is to be misrepresented, misjudged. So, let me be more precise: to live amongst others is either to be *mis*judged or to be judged and found wanting. — *Hell is other people.*

Sartre teaches me that life amongst others, life in hell, is a comedy of errors and manners; he teaches me to laugh at my predicament.

A Comedy of Errors. — Errors of mistaken identity inevitably arise from the fact that others identify me with the various disguises I put on. Like when a monarch, god, or angel disguises themself as a beggar, the joke is never on the noble being disguised as a base sort of being, but on those who fall for the disguise.

A Comedy of Manners. — Faux pas inevitably arise from the fact that I cannot help but wear my disguises poorly. When a monarch, god, or angel disguises themself as a beggar, they struggle to maintain the mannerisms proper to beggars because they cannot help being otherwise than what they are pretending to be. The queen disguised as a beggar will "break character" so to speak when the queen maintains her noble bearing, posture, and manner of speech while rebuffing the sexual advances of another beggar—the lecherous beggar will laugh at the queen for "pretending to be a lady", but all who know otherwise will laugh at the lecherous beggar who is incapable of recognizing nobility when it literally strikes him in the face.

Unlike the queen disguised as a beggar, however, I can be represented as *nothing* otherwise than what I am taken for. My poorly worn disguises betray nothing, just the fact that I am wanting, lacking. That being said, Sartre assures me that, like the queen is proud of the fact that she cannot help but represent nobility, I should be proud of the fact that I cannot help but represent nothing. Sartre inspires me to be rueful about everything that I have been taken to (mis)represent and smug about nothing.

Alas, Sartre also teaches me that life, tragically, is entirely a matter of representation.

No exit. — I am fated to betray nothing in one of two ways. Here and now, I bid others to misrepresent and misjudge me, deploying the stratagems of love and their kin, the stratagems of language, masochism. Then and there, I bid others to judge me and find me wanting, deploying the stratagems of desire and their kin, the stratagems of indifference, hate, sadism. Whichever way, it is my choice. So, let me be more precise: I am fated to choose a manner in which to betray nothing. — *No exit.*

To deny that I have choices in matters of representation, choices in life—this, Sartre teaches me, is *bad faith.*

Speaking in bad faith, whether I am misjudged or judged and found wanting, I say to my judges, "I am what I am, and I've got no choice in the matter. You should feel guilty for expecting otherwise from me. Oh, pity me or put me out of my misery!"

Speaking freely, I say to my judges, "I have made my choice, for better or for worse, and I shall be judged for it, but I care for neither your guilt nor your pity."

Sartre teaches me to live authentically, to live in a manner that involves speaking freely. It doesn't matter whether I choose the stratagems of love, the stratagems of desire, or any of their respective kin, all that matters is that the stratagems that I choose involve speaking freely over and against speaking in bad faith. For instance, I choose to live authentically when I choose a stratagem of love which involves saying, "Let us choose love in spite of everything!" By contrast, I choose to live inauthentically when I choose a stratagem of love which involves saying, "Our love cannot be helped: we are meant for each other!"

Fatal stratagems are those that involve speaking in bad faith; *vital stratagems* are those that involve speaking freely. These are, of course, my terms, not Sartre's, but Sartre teaches me to distinguish between the vital and the fatal and he inspires me to choose the vital over and against the fatal. This, for me, is Sartre's great lesson. — *An authentic choice is a vital betrayal of nothing.*

Deleuze teaches me that Sartre cedes too much too early when he accepts that life is entirely a matter of representation.

I can't be *represented* otherwise than a wanting, a lacking, a nothing, but why can't I *live* otherwise? To live amongst others who are motivated to (mis)represent me and to make me (mis)represent them—that, indeed, is hell. However, to live amongst others who motivate me to live otherwise and whom I motivate to live otherwise—this, no doubt, is heaven.

These others who are motivated to (mis)represent and to be (mis)represented, these others who would trick me into believing that life is entirely a matter of representation, who tricked Sartre— who are they and what motivates them? I call them *the exhausted*, for they are motivated by an exhaustion of forces.

The exhausted are those who put ends to things because they haven't any force to create themselves otherwise than they already are. They say, "Never again! Enough is enough! No more! That's that! There must be an end goal and a final solution!" For how can the exhausted cope with difference when they cannot create themselves otherwise than they already are? Lest they perish, the exhausted must arrange the world so that everything different is a (mis)representation of what they, the exhausted, already are: the exhausted must be the origin which anticipates the end, the end that recapitulates the origin, and the crucial turning point that discloses the origin and encloses the end. In other words, lest they perish, the exhausted must demonstrate an ability to put an end to everything different by (mis)representing all differences as marginal by-products of regularizing processes.

II. G. Deleuze

The "other" others, those who are motivated to live otherwise and who motivate me to live otherwise—who are they and what motivates them? I call them *exuberants*, for they are motivated by an exuberance of forces.

Exuberants eternally return, impelled by a superfluity of forces to create themselves otherwise than they are. They must go on, even when they can't go on, they go on schizophrenically creating themselves otherwise and, as a result, they ceaselessly become evermore irregular, evermore anomalous, evermore singular. Exuberants do not cope with difference: exuberants embody difference.

Following Nietzsche, Deleuze teaches me that the exhausted resent exuberants for being exuberant, they begrudge exuberants their exuberance. Encountering exuberance makes the exhausted bitterly aware of their exhaustion and, unfortunately for exuberants, rather than recognizing their own exhaustion as the true source of their bitterness, the exhausted make scapegoats of exuberants. The exhausted find the source of their bitterness in the exuberance of exuberants, and the exhausted commit themselves to putting an end to their bitterness by exhausting exuberants.

Q: How do the exhausted exhaust exuberants?

A: Guilt. Pity. Brutality.

Guilt. — The (mis)judgments of the exhausted compel exuberants to believe that exuberance is the vicious abuse of undeserved privileges. The exhausted preach, "Exuberance is evidence of a crime — against the Faith, against Humanity, against Nature, against the People, against the Family — a crime that must be uncovered and atoned for! Exhaustion is the only proof of atonement! Exhaust yourselves, exuberants, and atone for your crimes!"

Pity. — The (mis)judgments of the exhausted compel exuberants to believe that exhaustion is, for many, a grueling undertaking, pregnant with virtue and humility. The exhausted preach, "While you, pretentious and vain exuberants, advance your singularity, so many simple souls are struggling for regularity! Pity these simple souls struggling to achieve the least amount of dignity! Put your phantasmatic singularity aside and lend a helping hand to people dealing with regular problems."

Brutality. — When their (mis)judgments fail to inspire guilt and pity in exuberants, the exhausted employ (mis)judgments to justify slandering, raping, torturing, and killing exuberants.

History, as the exhausted tell it, is the history of the oft violent struggles between different factions of the exhausted over whose (mis)judgments are best at inspiring guilt and pity and whose are the best justifications for slandering, raping, torturing, and killing. Each and every monumental civilization that features in the histories of the exhausted is a mega-machine for enforcing a hierarchy of (mis)judgments, and the different protagonists of exhausted histories, the politicians and the priests, are champions of different hierarchies of (mis)judgments.

Exuberants who suffer from but do not fall victim to the (mis)judgments of the exhausted have nothing but contempt for the exhausted. *To have done with the judgment*, exuberants flee from the exhausted and endeavor to live a nomadic life of exile in a desert wilderness, wandering alongside others who've gone into self-imposed exile.

History, as exuberants tell it, is a haphazardly connected series of flights from civilization and the protagonists of exuberant histories are those who create motives for living otherwise than bidding (mis) representation and who create vital means for betraying nothing when being (mis)represented.

Alas, nothing makes the exhausted more bitterly aware of their exhaustion than the successful flight of exuberants into the wilderness. There must be *no exit*, no wilderness to escape to! So, the exhausted endeavor to domesticate all the wilds that they can and to lay waste to all the wilds that they cannot domesticate: the exhausted endeavor to civilize and surveil every habitable corner of the world so that, forevermore, no living creature can ever have done with judgment.

Hell is a sprawling network of civilized domains with no exit, where exuberants, having been misjudged or judged and found wanting, are guilted, made to feel to pity, and brutalized. Heaven is an exit, a line of flight to a guiltless and pitiless desert wilderness, an escape route along which exuberants, having done with judgment, encounter one another by creating themselves otherwise than they are.

Sartre wrote guidebooks for exuberants living in hell, trapped in sedentarizing enclosures of representation; Deleuze discovered and mapped escape routes for exuberants who would live freely as nomads on an open desert plane of immanence.

The vital stratagems of love, desire, and their respective kin, as described in Sartre's guidebooks, are *means* for betraying nothing in bidding (mis)representation. The tactical dis-organ-izations of desire mapped by Deleuze are *motives* for living otherwise than bidding (mis)representation.

I must have vital means for betraying nothing if I am to survive in hell, yes, but I must have motives for living otherwise if I am ever going to make a heavenly escape. Deleuze teaches me that, while betraying nothing may take phenomenological precedence over living otherwise, living otherwise takes ethical precedence over betraying nothing, and, following Spinoza, ethics is ontologically prior to phenomenology. This, for me, is Deleuze's great lesson: *motives for living otherwise precede vital means for betraying nothing.*

Solutions for

Postmodern Living

From M to Y:

3 June 2017

I have two great loves in my life: there is philosophy and there is you. You two have encountered one another often enough and I often speak to each of you of the other, but you two haven't gotten together of your own accord in order to truly get to know one another. It pains me to find that, despite the fact that my love for each of you is so overwhelming, you two don't have much of a relationship with each other. I am determined, however, to bring you two together, not just for my own sake, but for each other's sake. For I am certain that, once you two have gotten to know each other, you two will become magnificent friends. And who better to bring you two together than I, the one person who loves you both so deeply.

So, philosophy, allow me to formally introduce you to Y.

Y., allow me to formally introduce you to philosophy.

Y., philosophy has traditionally been the search for ultimate universal answers—that is, final, all-inclusive, and all-embracing answers—to fundamental metaphysical, epistemic, ethical, political, and aesthetic questions:

> *What is there?*
> *How does it appear?*
> *How can we know what there is and how it appears?*
> *What is good and what is bad for the individual? For society?*
> *What is beautiful and what is sublime?*
> *How do we distinguish the good from the bad?*
> *The beautiful from the sublime?*

Y., I am not interested in traditional philosophy, and I am not introducing you to traditional philosophy. Undoubtedly, I am interested in fundamental questions like those listed above, but I have no interest in finding the ultimate universal answers to them. The philosophy that I am enamored with and the philosophers whom I claim as my forbearers and hope to claim as my friends and followers are those who cast aspersions upon ultimate universal answers to fundamental questions.

Y., I would like to introduce you to transformative philosophy. Instead of seeking ultimate universal answers to fundamental questions, transformative philosophy seeks generative transversal answers.

Ultimate answers are final answers; lines of questioning are terminated once ultimate answers are found. *Generative answers* are initial answers; lines of questioning are initiated when generative answers are found.

Universal answers are all-inclusive and all-embracing they are unifying and totalizing; in other words, universal answers are totalitarian: they claim absolute authority, they aim to regulate every aspect of everything they touch, and they are intolerant towards all that would elude or escape them. *Transversal answers* are idiosyncratic, they are "unities that do not unify" and "totalities that do not totalize"; in other words, transversal answers are pluralist: they make no absolute claims to authority, they acknowledge the autonomy of everything that they touch, and they accept that persons and things can and will elude and escape them.

Y., it comes as no surprise to me that you were never eager to meet philosophy or spend much time with philosophy before now. Almost everyone's first introduction to philosophy is an introduction to traditional philosophy; those who are introduced to transformative philosophy are either fortunate to have great teachers or fortunate to have accidentally come into contact with transformative philosophy on their own.

Y., someone like you sees through traditional philosophy and traditional philosophers in an instant and has nothing more to do with them. Why would you want spend your time with traditional philosophers, a bunch of phallogocentric farts, neurotic mansplainers claiming to have reasoned insight into the ultimate universal answers to life's fundamental questions? Someone like you knows, without having to read a word of traditional philosophy, that ultimate universal answers to fundamental questions are recipes for oppression. So, when you hear the word philosophy, you're primed to reach for your gun, and justifiably so insofar as the term philosophy does indeed all too often refer to traditional philosophy.

Y., please allow me to introduce you to transformative philosophy, to philosophy as a phantastic form of storytelling, "in part a very special sort of detective story, in part a sort of science-fiction."

With love,
M.

From M to Y:

4 June 2017

You've crossed paths with a creature who looks a lot like transformative philosophy but who brings great sadness rather than great joy into the word. This rather unfortunate creature is transformative philosophy's bizarro doppelgänger, defeatist philosophy. Defeatist philosophy masquerades around the world in the guise of transformative philosophy, wreaking confusion and havoc everywhere it goes. I would lament this travesty at great length, but I know that you've met more than a few individuals who've been taken in by the ruses of defeatist philosophy and its enablers. You can easily guess why it is important to me that you don't confuse defeatist philosophy with transformative philosophy, but it won't hurt if I write a few words on this matter.

Defeatist philosophy mimics transformative philosophy's arguments against traditional philosophy and then misconstrues them in order to perpetuate an atmosphere of despair. Transformative philosophy and defeatist philosophy both agree that traditional philosophy's ultimate universal answers are totalitarian constructs, but defeatist philosophy goes on to draw the extreme conclusion that seeking answers in anyway whatsoever is a totalitarian endeavor. In other words, defeatist philosophy argues that anyone who would seek any kind of answer to a fundamental question must be an oppressor, and defeatist philosophy argues that "good" philosophy and "good" philosophers should spend their time calling out anyone and everyone who seeks answers to fundamental questions, "Oppressors!"

The Second Letter

More often than not, defeatist philosophy makes accurate claims: traditional philosophy prevails and traditional philosophy is oppressive. The problem is, of course, that defeatist philosophers plug their ears and roll their eyes with smug condescension when transformative philosophers point out that traditional philosopher's ultimate universal answers aren't the only possible answers to fundamental questions.

Y., I'm sure you have no trouble recognizing the fact that defeatist philosophy is a waste of time: you have zero tolerance for incessant naysayers, for those who love to play the passive role of the victim, for those who constantly protest but never create and discover. Transformative philosophy is different from defeatist philosophy. Unlike defeatist philosophy, transformative philosophy aims to say "yay" rather than "nay", it abhors and avoids playing the passive role of the victim, and it passes through protest as a means to create and discover.

With love,

M.

From M to Y:

5 June 2017,

It is unfortunate that I cannot introduce you to transformative philosophy without first remarking upon the fact that transformative philosophy differs from its relations, from its overbearing father, traditional philosophy, and from its bizarro twin sibling, defeatist philosophy. Alas, this can't be helped: when your father is a well-known reactionary and your twin sibling is a killjoy who vents their bad conscience in your name, introductions are always going to be a little bit awkward.

Luckily, I am introducing transformative philosophy to you, Y., and you are open minded and discerning. What's more, Y., you may sympathize with transformative philosophy's predicament. Transformative philosophy is a restless free spirit seeking to escape family legacies and live a life full of creativity and discovery, estranged from a parent and a sibling overly invested in a family legacy and its attendant dramas. You and transformative philosophy have shared experiences to bond over, compassion and counsel to give to one another, and shared problems you can work through together.

Transformative philosophy is desperate for friends like you, Y. You see, traditional philosophy seeks answers to fundamental questions for everyone: it aims to make a place for everyone and put everyone in their rightful place. Transformative philosophy doesn't seek to answer fundamental questions for everyone, but only for people like you, it seeks answers to fundamental questions that would empower people like you—people who refuse to remain "in their place", no matter how comfortable and happy they would be if they chose to remain. Transformative philosophy is for all those who would escape the legacies of their family, their nation, their race, their class, their religion, their gender and, above all else, their very own personal legacy in order to live a life full of creativity and discovery.

Y., have ever I told you the *Allegory of the Sea Squirt*? Starting off as an egg, the sea squirt quickly develops into a tadpole-like creature, complete with a spinal cord connected to a simple eye and a tail for swimming. It also has a brain that it uses to locomote through the water. But the sea squirt's mobility doesn't last long. Once it finds a suitable place to attach itself, whether it is to the hull of a boat, underwater rocks, or the ocean floor, it never moves again. Indeed, once the sea squirt has attached itself to a suitable place, the sea squirt will consume and shit away its twitching tail, consume and shit away its primitive eye and spinal cord, and consume and shit away the brain that it used to find a suitable attachment place. You see, once it has found and attached itself to a suitable place, the sea squirt's tail, eye, spinal cord, and brain become superfluous burdens that need to be disposed of.

Y., traditional philosophers, along with those to whom traditional philosophy consciously or unconsciously appeals, are sea squirts: once they find their ultimate universal answers to the fundamental questions, any further exercise of reason or intuition with regard to fundamental questions is a superfluous burden for them; they will consume and shit away the organs that enabled them to think about fundamental questions and they will advise others like them to do the same.

Transformative philosophers, and those to whom transformative philosophy consciously or unconsciously appeals, are creatures that could never find and will never search for a suitable attachment place: they continually maintain and work to strengthen the organs that allow them to think about the fundamental questions and they advise others like them to do the same.

With love,

M.

From M to Y:

6 June 2017

We've discussed traditional philosophy, transformative philosophy's overbearing father, and we've discussed defeatist philosophy, transformative philosophy's bizarro twin sibling, but we've yet to discuss critical philosophy, transformative philosophy's self-righteous younger sibling. Traditional philosophy has prevailed in most times and places, but critical philosophy prevails in our time amongst the WEIRD: the Western(ized), Educated, Industrialized, Rich, and Democratic.

You already know that traditional philosophy seeks ultimate universal answers to fundamental questions and that transformative philosophy seeks generative transversal answers. I should like to remark upon how defeatist philosophy seeks ultimate transversal answers to fundamental questions and how critical philosophy seeks generative universal answers. A brief recap:

> Ultimate answers *are final answers; lines of questioning are terminated once ultimate answers are found.* Generative answers *are initial answers; lines of questioning are initiated when generative answers are found.*

> Universal answers *are all-inclusive and all-embracing, they are unifying and totalizing; in other words, universal answers are totalitarian: they claim absolute authority, they aim to regulate every aspect of everything they touch, and they are intolerant towards all that would elude or escape them.* Transversal answers *are idiosyncratic, they are 'unities that do not unify' and 'totalities that do not totalize'; in other words, transversal answers are pluralist: they make no absolute claims to authority, they respect the autonomy of everything that they touch, and they accept that persons and things can and will elude and escape them.*

Traditional philosophy, which seeks ultimate universal answers, seeks to terminate lines of questioning with all-inclusive and all-embracing answers—which is to say, traditional philosophy seeks to put everyone and everything in their proper place and make sure that everyone and everything stays settled in their proper place. In seeking answers to fundamental questions, the traditional philosopher is, at bottom, seeking an answer to the following question, "How can I put a given person or thing in its proper place and keep them there?"

The Fourth Letter

Transformative philosophy, which seeks generative transversal answers, seeks to initiate lines of questioning with idiosyncratic answers—which is to say, transformative philosophy seeks to give everyone and everything the freedom to travel to anyplace and settle anyplace along an original path. In seeking answers to fundamental questions, the transformative philosopher is, at bottom, seeking an answer to the following question, "Can I facilitate the invention of new and unusual ways to get a given person or thing from one place to another?"

Defeatist philosophy, which seeks ultimate transversal answers, seeks to terminate lines of questioning with idiosyncratic answers—which is to say, defeatist philosophy gives everyone and everything the freedom to travel anyplace while denying them the freedom to settle anyplace. In seeking answers to fundamental questions, the defeatist philosopher is, at bottom, seeking an answer to the following question, "How can I prevent a given person or thing from ever settling in any one place?"

Critical philosophy, which seeks generative universal answers, seeks to initiate lines of questioning with all-inclusive and all-embracing answers—which is to say, critical philosophy seeks to limit the travel and settlement of everyone and everything by assigning everyone and everything a proper channel of communication and transportation. In seeking answers to fundamental questions, the critical philosopher is primarily seeking an answer to the following questions, "What is the right way for a given person or thing to go from one place to another?"

Y., critical philosophy, like traditional philosophy, is totalitarian, but critical philosophy unifies and totalizes in a different manner than traditional philosophy does. Traditional philosophy unifies and totalizes as the arbiter of the facts: traditional philosophy will tell you as a matter of fact (*quid facti*) the who, what, where, why, and how of persons and things. Critical philosophy doesn't unify and totalize as the arbiter of the facts but, rather, as the arbiter of rights: critical philosophy will tell you as a matter of law (*quid juris*) whether or not the who, what, where, why, and how of persons and things are right, justified. Critical philosophy is open to the facts changing as long as the rules that govern the facts remain fixed, whereas traditional philosophy wants to permanently fix both the facts and the rules governing the facts—therein lies the difference between the generative universal and the ultimate universal.

With love,

M.

From M to Y:

7 June 2017

Transformative philosophy is not for everyone and it doesn't pretend to be for everyone.

> *Transformative philosophy is not for* traditional conformers, *not for people who have found their place in the world and plan to live out the rest of their lives in their place, who reason or sense that life has a definite, fixed outcome.*

> *Transformative philosophy is not for* traditional reformers, *not for people who are searching for a place in the world where they can live out the rest of their lives, who reason or sense that life should eventually reach a definite, fixed outcome.*

> *Transformative philosophy is not for* critical conformers, *not for people who have an established set of rules instructing them on how to live their lives, who reason or sense that life is a game with fixed rules that limit possible outcomes and render certain outcomes inaccessible.*

> *Transformative philosophy is not for* critical reformers, *not for people who seek to establish a set of rules that will instruct them on how to live their lives, who reason or sense that life should eventually become a game with fixed rules that limit possible outcomes and render certain outcomes inaccessible.*

> *Transformative philosophy is not for* deformers, *not for people who reason or sense that life is a meaningless chaos with no fixed outcome and no limits to possible outcomes.*

Y., transformative philosophy is for *transformers*. Who is a transformer, you ask? When we are at our best, you and I are transformers—or, at the very least, I am certain that we strive to be. More generally, however, there are three characteristics that define a transformer:

> *1. A transformer is someone who reasons or senses that life is a momentary achievement snatched from chaos, that life is meaningful order emerging from chaos for a time, not for all time;*

2. A transformer is someone who reasons or senses that the processes through which life emerges from chaos are the only factors that can limit the possible outcomes of life and, although these processes may occasionally display patterns, these processes do not abide by any rules; and

3. A transformer is someone who aims to influence the processes through which life emerges from chaos in ways that increase life's possible outcomes, rendering more outcomes accessible for themselves and for others.

Put these three characteristics together and a transformer can be defined in the following manner: *a transformer is someone who braves chaos in order to create and discover new possibilities of life.*

Now, isn't the transformer a grand character, the character that you've always imagined yourself to be, the character that you still strive to be, in spite of all the dangers that such a character must face?

Y., transformative philosophy is not for everyone because not everyone is or wants to be a transformer, and because transformers aren't interested in forcing everyone to be like them. To force everyone to become a transformer is to limit life's possible outcomes, and that runs counter to the transformer's *modus vivendi.* That being said, transformers are still the enemies of those who would decrease life's possible outcomes: they subvert the machinations of conformers and reformers and they dismiss the defeatism of deformers. So, transformative philosophy addresses non-transformers to no end, often in an antagonistic manner, but only for the sake of transformers.

With love,

M.

From M to Y:

8 June 2017

Transformers, in braving chaos to create and discover new possibilities of life, will always embody a transformative philosophy, but, because transformative philosophies are not readily available to them, many transformers find that they must betray a traditional, critical, or defeatist philosophy to become the transformers they are. Transformers who betray non-transformative philosophies can only create and discover new possibilities of life with a bad conscience.

Transformative philosophy aims to give transformers an understanding and a sensibility for metaphysical, epistemological, ethical, political, and aesthetic problems that would allow them to create and discover new possibilities of life without a bad conscience. Without transformative philosophy, transformers must perform elaborate rituals of self-deception in order to encourage themselves to brave chaos and they must perform elaborate rituals of self-flagellation in order to atone for the crime of realizing new possibilities of life that run counter to traditional, critical, or defeatist philosophies. Transformative philosophy aims to liberate transformers from the need to self-deceive and self-flagellate, the need that non-transformative philosophies foist upon transformers.

Y., the profound problem here is that no human being, no specimen of a "symbolic species", can escape philosophy. Creatures who live with and through language must in some way account for the oppositions between the good and the bad, the beautiful and the ugly, the real and the imagined. Insofar as we account for such distinctions with and through language, we must, implicitly or explicitly, make some fundamental metaphysical, epistemic, ethical, political, and aesthetic observations.

All of us are trained by our societies to observe certain philosophies from a very young age, but I know of no one trained to observe a transformative philosophy as a child. Everyone I know, you and I included , has been trained to observe a traditional or critical philosophy of some kind.

Some free themselves from the traditional or critical philosophy that they were trained to observe only to retain a traditional or critical mindset and seek out or invent new traditional or critical philosophies.

Some free themselves from their traditional and critical mindsets only to develop a defeatist mindset and seek out or invent defeatist philosophies to guide them.

Some free themselves from traditional and critical mindsets, avoid or overcome a defeatist mindset, and develop a transformative mindset, but do not seek out or invent a transformative philosophy, either because they are daunted by or disillusioned with the enterprise of philosophy.

Without a transformative philosophy, however, individuals with a transformative mindset must either (i) stick with a traditional or critical philosophy and acquiesce to self-deception and self-flagellation, (ii) stick with a defeatist philosophy that allows one to openly condemn self-deception and self-flagellation while simultaneously engaging in self-deception and self-flagellation, or (iii) schizophrenically assume a host of different traditional, critical, and defeatist philosophies and play them against each other in order to ward off self-deception and self-flagellation as best one can.

Whatever the case may be, only a few transformers, the luckiest among us, can make do with non-transformative philosophies: only a few transformers can master the art of self-deception and endure regular self-flagellation while maintaining their capacity to create and discover new possibilities of life. Most transformers either cannot deceive themselves well enough or cannot endure constant self-flagellation; most transformers without a transformative philosophy succumb to self-deception and self-flagellation and lose their capacity to create and discover new possibilities of life, becoming miserable people as a result. Indeed, for a few years, I myself believed philosophy a lost cause and I resigned myself to inevitable exhaustion and misery.

With love,

M.

From M to Y:

Let's say that one wants to live a good life. How can one know whether or not one lives a good life if one has not asked oneself the question, "What is a good life?"

Let's say that one asks oneself the question, "What is a good life?" How does one go about finding an answer to that question? Does one seek answers from one's parents? From a priest? From a great philosopher-sage (in)famous for having answered the question? How does one know that any answer proffered by another is a good and true answer?

Let's say that one comes to the conclusion that one cannot trust any answer to the question of the good life except for one's own. How does one go about answering the question on one's own? Does one simply trust one's impulses? What if one's impulses pull in many different directions and give contradictory answers to the question? Can one harmonize the differences between one's impulses through exercise of reason? What if one's impulses cannot be harmonized? Can the exercise of reason help one determine which of one's impulses point in the right direction and which point in the wrong direction? What if there is no rational basis for making a judgment as to which impulses are right and which are wrong? What then?

Well, there you have it, my love, the course of my philosophical development, from the age of 13 to the age of 25, in brief. There were starts and stops, of course. It was not a steady progression from one question to the next. Along the way, there were great leaps forward, forced retreats, missteps, and stumbles. By age 25, however, I had planted my feet firmly where I left off above: I was at the edge of the cliff, looking down into the abyss, asking myself the question, "What then?"

I stood at that precipice looking into the void for over two years. I lived and loved during that time—I lived and loved a great deal, in fact—but my quest for a good life had come to a standstill. These were the most wretched years of my life: there were pleasures, yes, but I didn't know how to enjoy them. I felt as if I had lost myself.

Y., you know that old joke I like to tell about René Descartes.

> *Descartes walks into a bar. He orders a shot of whiskey. The bartender serves it up. Descartes downs it. The bartender asks, "Do you want another?"*

> *"No," Descartes replies, "I think not." And, right then and there, Descartes vanishes, he ceases to exist.*

A silly joke, yes, but it means so much to me. *Cogito, sum. Je pense, je suis.* I think, I am.

Descartes, having pursued doubt to the utmost extreme, stood on the edge of a cliff, looked down into the abyss, said to himself, "Je pense, je suis," and, like magic, the words that came out of his mouth formed a tightrope over the void which Descartes then traversed into the unknown.

It dawned on me one morning, laughing at that silly little joke in the shower, that Descartes's *Cogito* was just the magic spell I needed. "I think, I am" is not the epistemological proposition that professors of philosophy take it for. "I think, I am" is a grand expression that encapsulates the good life for those who would, like Descartes, pursue doubt to the utmost extreme. For me, "I think, I am" is not the universal truth upon which all knowledge is secured but, rather, it is a true expression of Descartes' lived experience, of my lived experience, of the lived experience of all those who give utmost primacy to those impulses that drive them to hyperbolically doubt—we, the few who feel strongly and deeply that our existence would have no basis if we ceased thinking, we who would rather not be than not think, we for whom the following epitaph would be a supreme triumph: *we thought, we were.*

There is no rational basis upon which I can say with any degree of certainty which of my impulses are right and which are wrong with regard to the question of the good life. That being said, however, I must acknowledge the irrational primacy of the impulses that have driven me to ask said question and to answer said question for myself. Just recall how I felt as if I had lost myself at the very moment that I reached the edge of the cliff and could not think any further about the question of the good life. Indeed, hadn't what happened to Descartes in my silly joke actually happened to me? I had stopped thinking about the question of the good life and it was as if I had stopped existing altogether.

A bad life for me would be a life in which the question of the good life was never asked, a life in which answers to the question of the good life is taken for granted, a life in which one must always look to others for answers and refrain from thinking for oneself, a life in which the question of the good life is asked and answered once and for all (*quid juris* and/or *quid facti*).

For me, a good life is a life in which one continually asks oneself the question of the good life, dreams up idiosyncratic hypotheses regarding the good life, and translates these idiosyncratic hypotheses into experiments with one's own life.

Y., transformative philosophy lets me give utmost primacy to those impulses driving me to endlessly approach the question of the good life with idiosyncratic, conditional hypotheses and to translate these hypotheses into experiments with one's own life.

With love,

M.

"The confrontation of the philosopher-honest man with the philosopher-villain goes back to Plato." Pierre Klossowski writes, "The philosopher-honest man avails himself of the act of thinking as the sole valid activity of his being. The villain who philosophizes does not grant thought any value other than favoring the activity of the strongest passion—which in the eyes of the honest man is never anything but a lack of being. If the supreme villainy consists of disguising one's passion as thought, the villain for his part never finds in the thought of an honest man anything but the disguise of an impotent passion."

Every living philosopher is a villain: the only true philosopher-honest man would be a corpse. Traditional and critical philosophers, insofar as they live, are simply dishonest about their villainy: the philosopher-honest man is a disguise that traditional and critical philosophers wear in order to conceal their strongest passions from others, including themselves. Traditional and critical philosophers rationalize because they are ashamed of acting according to their strongest passions; they use reason to excuse actions in line with their strongest passions. "I do this not because I am impelled to," traditional and critical philosophers lie to us, "I do this because reason dictates that I do this: you cannot argue against reason."

What is most fascinating about Socrates is not the fact that he was a true philosopher-honest man—he wasn't—but the fact that the activity of his strongest passion was, paradoxically, the activity of thinking. Socrates was a villain, just like every other philosopher, but villainy of his sort gets as close as villainy can ever get to honesty. The proximity of Socrates' villainy to honesty enabled Socrates to lose himself most completely in his own deceptions and enables us to lose ourselves most completely in Socrates' deceptions. Unlike lesser philosophers who claim to be compelled by reason but are in fact compelled by a passion for something other than reason and instrumentalize reason in order to affirm the sovereignty of a passion for something other than reason—Socrates was compelled by a passion for reason: he instrumentalized reason in order to affirm the sovereignty of his passion for reason. Note, however, that a passion for reason is different from reason itself: it is all too easy, and all too human, to confuse the two, and Socrates, wittingly or unwittingly, promoted this confusion.

Socrates did something else that was all too easy and all too human: Socrates argued that everyone should be just like him. Socrates universalized from his own experience and argued that reason is the source of all virtue and virtue, in turn, is the source of all happiness. Socrates' villainous philosophy was legitimized by the fact that it was so much closer to honesty than the villainous philosophies of contemporary rivals, the so-called Sophists, and this mode of legitimation has lent staying power to Socrates' villainous philosophy through the ages.

1. Socrates

What's more, from the Socratic vantage point, from the point at which villainy comes closest to honesty, one can speculate about the "truth" of the philosopher-honest man in such a way that enables one to disparage the philosopher-villain with a good deal of persuasive force—and this is exactly what Socrates did. Exhausted critics who remark upon Nietzsche's hatred of Socrates are remarking upon Nietzsche's revulsion at Socrates for having instigated the false war between the "good" philosopher-honest men and the "evil" philosopher villains that has sapped the energies of greater philosophers for millennia.

Socrates had his failings, yes, but I consider him a most remarkable historical personage because he is so well regarded amongst those who acutely demonstrate that which, according to my understanding, is the only common characteristic of my people, the greater philosophers: we greater philosophers can only be characterized by the fact that the activity of our strongest passions is the activity of thinking. Note, however, that the strongest passions of greater philosophers differ widely: it is only the activity of our strongest passions—that is, the activity through which we come to habitually discharge our strongest passions—that we have in common. It is only for the sake of convenience that I use the phrase "a passion for reason" to refer to so many disparate passions that are afforded profound discharge by the activity of thinking. Socrates' passion(s) for reason, Descartes' passion(s) for reason, and Nietzsche's passion(s) for reason each differ from one another and this accounts for so many philosophical differences between these three greater philosophers.

Legend has it that Socrates was a keen student of nature as a young man but gave up the study of nature, with its mutable and eternally changing forms, for the study of the realm of ideas, with its immutable and eternally fixed forms. In other words, Socrates abandoned the study of generative transversal forms for the study of ultimate universal forms. Curiously enough, what Socrates discovered everywhere he went was that so many forms celebrated as ultimate universals were, in fact, only generative transversals that had been given airs and graces by the sophistry of some philosopher villain. Yet, despite his continual re-discovery that ultimate universals were never what they appeared to be, Socrates, as we know him from Plato, was not lead to conclude that the realm of ideas was a continuation of the natural world, a realm of mutable and eternally changing forms, a realm of generative transversals. Why did Socrates' belief in a realm of ultimate universals persist despite so much evidence to the contrary? Did Socrates' belief in ultimate universals actually persist or was Diogenes right: did Plato, who tells us that Socrates maintained a belief in ultimate universals, misrepresent Socrates?

Philosophy & Villainy:

To refute Zeno of Elea, Parmenides' most celebrated follower, who argued that multiplicity and motion are illusions that do not follow from any necessity, Diogenes the Cynic simply stood up and went for a walk.

Traditional and critical philosophers have heaped scorn upon Diogenes for refuting an argument with an action: such a refutation shows no regard for the mechanics of Zeno's arguments, and to disregard the mechanics of another philosopher's arguments is unbecoming of the philosopher honest-man: it is a mark of shameless villainy. Diogenes, for his part, spent a good many daylight hours walking through the assemblies and marketplaces of Athens holding a lighted lamp up to the faces of the people he encountered there, searching for, but never finding, an honest man.

Transformative philosophers celebrate Diogenes, the philosopher cum performance artist, a singular dissembler of "the unity of life and thought … a unity that turns an anecdote of life into an aphorism of thought and an evaluation of thought into a new perspective on life." Parmenides and Zeno are opponents of the unity of life and thought: they oppose thought to life and they negate the reality of life in favor the reality of thought. In life, we never encounter a single timeless, necessary Being: we only ever encounter so many superfluous beings, so many untimely swerves into and out of being. We may approach a timeless, necessary Being through the activity of thinking, yes, but how is approaching such a Being in thought a refutation of all the beings that we encounter in life? Transformative philosophers turn away from Parmenides, Zeno, and all those like them who would claim that a Being approached in thought is a legitimate refutation of beings encountered in life.

There is no reason for us to refute the beings we encounter in life by privileging the Being we approach in thought, yes, but the reverse is also true: there is also no reason for us to refute the Being we approach in thought by privileging the beings that we encounter in life. This latter point, the flip side of the coin, inspires the transformative philosopher to turn towards Parmenides and Zeno. Parmenides and Zeno are anathemas to me insofar as they would use thought to refute life but they are my friends, or the enemies of my enemies at least, insofar as they are the enemies of those who would use life to refute thought.

2. Parmenides

So, let us return to Diogenes' walk, a most egregious act of villainous philosophizing. What all greater philosophers strive to achieve, is the unity of life and thought, a life that affirms thought and a thought that affirms life in circle. But what kind of circle: that is the question: the virtuous circle of the sham(ed) philosopher-honest man or the vicious circle of the shameless philosopher villain? Diogenes' villainous walk does not refute the thought that refutes life; it only refutes the refutation of life. Diogenes's walk affirms the fact that life and thought are different but, at the same time, it enables life and thought to become one another in turn.

One can still argue that multiplicity and motion do not exist after Diogenes' walk, but one continually re-encounters multiplicity and motion when one considers Diogenes' walk as a response to arguments against the existence of multiplicity and motion: whenever we consider the anecdote of Diogenes' walk we find that an encounter with multiplicity and motion becomes thought and, subsequently, we find that thought becomes an encounter with multiplicity and motion but, strangely, the encounter with multiplicity and motion becomes the thought that thought differs from the lived encounter, and thought becomes a lived encounter affirming the fact that thought differs from life. Yes, here we have it: the unity of life and thought in a vicious circle—life becoming thought in such a way that heightens the difference between life and thought and, vice versa, thought becoming life in such a way that heightens the difference between life and thought. By contrast, the unity of life and thought in a virtuous circle would drive thought and life to become less and less different from one another and more and more alike.

Philosophy & Villainy:

Heraclitus, the riddler, the obscure, the exponent of an order that subsists on ceaseless change, a misanthrope who broke from society to wander the mountains and live in solitude—a transformative philosopher if there ever was one. "I sought for myself," Heraclitus tells us, and this is the One thing that transformative philosophers ever tell—otherwise, transformative philosophers tell many things.

Heraclitus sought for himself and found fire, but he didn't start the fire: it was always burning. Heraclitus' God, the ever-living, ever-changing fire that Heraclitus found when he sought for himself, isn't the creator of the Cosmos but, rather, the continual recreation of the Cosmos: the only thing constant: change. The Abrahamic God—that is, God the Creator, the constancy of an ultimate beginning—has nothing to do with the God of Heraclitus, and the God of Heraclitus would have nothing to do with the Abrahamic God except burn Him and His Creation to ash.

To recreate the thought of Heraclitus is to play with fire; to play with fire is to burn; to burn is to be transformed. Heraclitus entreats us, "Burn baby burn!", and he weeps because so few are willing to play with fire, so many would rather quench fires for good.

Plato is the great exponent of the unity of life and thought in a virtuous circle. Plato holds that ultimate universals, the singular immutable forms that we approach in thought, are true forms; generative transversals, the plurality of mutable forms that we encounter in life, are but corruptions of true forms. Plato sought to put an end the corruption of true forms: there is a circular process, he argued, through which the plurality of mutable forms that we encounter in life could come to accurately resemble the singular immutable forms that we approach in thought—this process is dialectical reason and the result of this process is justice. The philosopher-honest man is he who engages dialectical reason, ergo the philosopher-honest man is he who institutes justice. If we want a just world the philosopher-honest man must rule it.

The basic argument of Plato's *Republic* can be summarized quite briefly and neatly, as above, but the *Republic* is more than this basic argument—the *Republic* is itself a demonstration of the process of dialectical reason that it argues for: in other words, the *Republic* would "do justice" to its own argument.

I hold that every living philosopher is a villain and the philosopher-honest man is no more than a disguise that some villains wear to conceal their strongest passions from others, including themselves. I could demonstrate that Plato doesn't "do justice" to his own argument in the *Republic* and that his failure to do so betrays his villainous philosophy. Alas, I haven't the will to engage in such a tedious exercise and the conclusions of such an exercise seem rather obvious: Plato had a passion for ruling but what Plato excelled at was thinking; Plato argued that the best rulers were the best thinkers so that his great talent for thinking would affirm his passion for ruling.

Those who have both a passion for ruling and the greater talent for ruling are too busy ruling or trying to rule to give so much thought to thought. Those who have a passion for ruling but the greater talent for thinking will think a great deal about how thought can affirm their passion for ruling. Plato was a talented thinker who would be a ruler and Plato appeals to other talented thinkers who would be rulers. Do not count Plato and Platonists among my people, among the greater philosophers, for their strongest passion is a passion for ruling, not for thinking. Plato and Platonists instrumentalize thought, transforming thought into a means to formulate and enforce rules and regulations.

4. Plato

Diogenes the Cynic performed a number of philosophical stunts at Plato's expense that betrayed Plato's stature as a lesser philosopher. "Rule:" Plato told his Academy, "Man, true to form, is defined as an animal, biped and featherless." Diogenes plucked a fowl, brought it into Plato's lecture-room and exclaimed, "Here is Plato's man." In consequence of which the Academics, in accordance with dialectical reason, added to the definition, "having broad nails." – This is Plato's justice and this is what amounts to justice for so many: either by the thoughtful action of a Diogenes or by chance occurrence, the fallacy of a given rule is betrayed: this betrayal is called injustice and justice must be re-established according to dialectical reason by amending the rule so as to better disguise the fallacy. The totalitarian state that Plato called a just society in the *Republic* ensures the perpetuation of justice and prevents injustice by outlawing thoughtful action by those who are not philosopher-honest men and putting an end to all chance occurrences, this way the fallacy of a given rule is never betrayed.

Alfred North Whitehead tells us, "The safest general characterization of the European philosophical tradition is that it consists of a series of footnotes to Plato." I do not entirely disagree with Whitehead: every trick in the lesser philosophers' play-book can be traced back to Plato. If you eschew "the safest general characterization", if you would rather play with fire, Plato is your enemy and you would best read and understand Plato in order to know your enemy.

Philosophy & Villainy:

5. The Stoics

The finest of the Stoics were greater philosophers who, after the manner of Socrates, lost themselves in their own deceptions, in pursuit of a phantasm: the philosopher-honest man. The Stoics, seeking to become philosopher-honest men, claimed to be freeing themselves from their passions and following reason by way of their askēsis, their asceticism, but these villainous philosophers were, in actual practice, letting their fiery, all-consuming passion for reason burn every other passion that would drive them.

The Stoics are worth reading because their teachings are justifications of their practices and, thus, make reference to and describe their practices. I disregard the Stoics' justifications of their practices—a passion for playing with fire is the only justification for putting out fire with gasoline. Instead, I recreate and re-purpose the Stoics' practices to no end and appreciate their talent for playing with fire.

Chief among the Stoics' askēsis are those that cultivate apathy, but, again, remember that apathy, in practice, is not the quenching of all passion but, rather, enabling one passion, the passion for reason, to engulf every other passion. Another way of putting it: imagine that your various passions constitute an ecosystem, Stoic practices are a sort of ecological engineering aiming to transform heterotrophic passion(s) for reason into the keystone species on which all other passions in an ecosystems largely depend. Stoic practices would have you become indifferent to speciations and extinctions of all passions other than passion(s) for reason unless such speciations and extinctions adversely affect the conservation of your passion(s) for reason.

The Stoics are traditional philosophers by my estimation because they would *conserve* passion(s) for reason, they would conserve the Tyger burning bright in the forests of the night. The Stoic seeks an immortal hand or eye that would endlessly conserve the Tyger's fearful symmetry. By contrast, the transformative philosopher, with their own mortal hands and eyes, dares to catalyze endless transformations of the Tyger's fearful symmetry. Transformative philosophers are as indifferent as Stoics to passions other than passion(s) for reason, but, instead of facilitating conservation like the Stoics, they would facilitate speciations, they would have passion(s) for reason become otherwise: how many ways can a passion for reason diversify in order to fill new niches and fill existing niches vacated by other passions gone extinct?

Philosophy & Villainy:

6. The Epicureans

"Physical desire is a sensual experience," Rainer Maria Rilke tells us, "no different from pure contemplation or the pure sensation with which a fine fruit sates the tongue." Contemplation affirmed as a sensual experience, as the indulgence of a passion, just like copulation and gustation—this is one of Rilke's most Epicurean affirmations.

The Epicureans, unlike the Stoics, did not pretend to quench their fiery passions through the exercise reason. To the contrary, the Epicureans, much to the Stoics' chagrin, openly admitted to indulging their passions through the exercise reason. To their discredit, however, the Epicureans were so ready to openly admit their indulgences because their indulgences were far less frightening than those of the Stoics. The asceticism of the Stoics conserved wild passions for reason in volatile wildernesses; the hedonism of the Epicureans nurtured domesticated passions for reason in tranquil gardens. A Stoic's passion for reason was a ferocious wolf; an Epicurean's passion for reason was a friendly dog.

Transformative philosophers openly admit to indulging their passion for reason like Epicureans but they are no more Epicureans in practice than they are Stoics. Transformative philosophers re-purpose or, even better, de-purpose the asceticism of the Stoics and the hedonism of the Epicureans to no end, to recreate without end, to catalyze endless speciations of wild passions for reason in dissimulated wildernesses. Engaged in such recreations, transformative philosophers may admit one of Rilke's most Stoic affirmations, "Strife is our closest companion."

Philosophy & Villainy:

7. The Skeptics

If the skeptic is defined by their choice to eschew the universal and affirm the transversal, the defeatist philosopher and the transformative philosopher are united under the banner of skepticism. To distinguish between a defeatist philosopher and a transformative philosopher, between a shameful skeptic-honest man and a shameless skeptic villain, I ask, "Does the skeptic's affirmation of the transversal put an end to rational inquiry or does it initiate new lines rational inquiry?"

The strongest passion of the defeatist philosopher, of the shameful skeptic-honest man, is not their passion for reason but, rather, a passion at odds with their passion for reason. The defeatist philosopher seeks to put an end to rational inquiry because the activity of rational inquiry impedes some other activity that they deem more vital. When one's passion for reason is too strong to be subjugated and instrumentalized by another passion, even though that other passions is stronger, one learns to play one's passion for reason against itself so as to advantage the other, stronger passion. The shameful skeptic-honest man is always a near-great philosopher: their passion for reason is a force that must be reckoned with by whatever other passion would drive them, but their passion for reason is not the passion that drives them.

So, the defeatist philosopher, the shameful skeptic-honest man, reasons that reason neither establishes knowledge nor virtue so that they may gleefully cease reasoning and follow a passion other than their passion for reason. By contrast, the transformative philosopher, the shameless skeptic-villain, is defiantly driven by their passion for reason: they reason that reason neither establishes knowledge nor virtue and, then, they gleefully continue to reason in spite of their reasoning, for no reason, without reason.

A further contrast, against the skeptics, traditional and critical philosophers, be they greater or lesser, reason that reason does establish knowledge and virtue in accord with their strongest passion (which may or may not be a passion for reason) and they proceed to follow their strongest passions under the cover of reason. Finally, the furthest contrast, against all philosophers, the non-philosopher simply follows their strongest passion without ever bothering to think about reason's relationship to knowledge and virtue, taking it for granted that their strongest passions are reasonable and, thus, virtuous.

The skeptic honest-man is not a "real" honest man but a disguise that a dishonest thinker wears in order to play their passion for reason against itself to the advantage another, stronger passion. The skeptic-villain, also a dishonest thinker, reasons against reason only to keep reasoning against reason, wherefore, in turn, the reasons for their acts and their acts of reasoning become increasingly different from one another in a viciously circular affirmation of their passion for reason.

Philosophy & Villainy:

Perhaps Mark Rothko could have said, "I paint, I am. I do not doubt myself when I paint—I cannot." Perhaps Pina Bausch could have said, "I dance, I am. I do not doubt myself when I dance—I cannot." Perhaps, but why would they have bothered? Their aesthetic practices dissimulated such epistemo-ontological statements.

The philosopher's aesthetic practice involves formulating epistemo-ontological statements: it is a joy, not a bother, for the philosopher to formulate such statements. René Descartes, whom I count among the greatest of greater philosophers, stated things most boldly, "*Cogito, sum.* I think, I am. I do not doubt myself when I think—I cannot." The philosopher-honest man will concede or refute Descartes' *Cogito*, as if the *Cogito* were a universal model of truth and not the expression of Descartes' strongest passion. The philosopher villain betrays Descartes' *Cogito*, exposing the fact that the *Cogito* is nothing but a transversal simulacra of the phantasms that haunt greater philosophers.

A greater painter, like Rothko, doubts themself when they engage in any activity that does not heighten the activity of painting: a greater painter will think deeply so as to paint passionately and will abandon thinking when thinking leads to passionless painting.

A greater dancer, like Bausch, doubts themself when they engage in any activity that does not heighten the activity of dancing: a greater dancer will think deeply so as to dance passionately and will abandon thinking when thinking leads to passionless dancing.

A greater philosopher, like Descartes, doubts themself when they engage in any activity that does not heighten the activity of thinking: a greater philosopher will dance, or paint, or feast, or fuck so as to think more passionately and they will abandon dancing, painting, feasting, and fucking when those activities lead to passionless thinking.

When one reads Descartes one must understand that every statement that he claims is immediately clear, distinctive, and self-evident is not a rational truth, as Descartes might have you believe, but, rather, an irrational fetish that heightens the activity of thinking for Descartes, and, what's more, contrary to what Descartes might have you believe, one should not take it for granted that those fetishes that heighten the activity of thinking for Descartes are those that heighten the activity of thinking for any other greater philosophers, or for lesser philosophers, or for non-philosophers. Descartes searches for himself and himself alone; one may or may not find affinities with Descartes in one's own search for oneself.

If you would love and be loved by a greater philosopher, it is not imperative that you share their strongest passion, their passion for reason. Rather, what is imperative is that loving you and being loved by you heightens the activity of thinking for the philosopher you would take for a lover: the statement, "I love you," should become an irrational fetish that heightens the activity of thinking for your lover. Vice versa, if a greater philosopher would love a greater thespian, for instance, the philosopher will learn to love and be loved by the thespian in a manner that heightens the activity that defines the thespian: acting.

Following from the above, let us imagine a viciously circular love affair between a greater philosopher and a greater thespian, their passions continually differing from, deferring to, and redoubling each other: the philosopher discovers ways in which thinking can heighten acting for the thespian; in return, the thespian discovers ways in which acting can heighten thinking for the philosopher; in return, the philosopher discovers more ways in which thinking can heighten acting for the thespian; in return, the thespian discovers more ways in which acting can heighten thinking for the philosopher; in return, …

Philosophy & Villainy:

9. Spinoza

My strongest passion is the passion which, when indulged, arouses the highest degree of joy in me and, when inhibited, the highest degree of sadness in me. The joy that I experience when I indulge my strongest passion cannot be dissociated from the strife between the different passions coursing through me: the strife that allows my strongest passion to prove that it is, indeed, stronger than my other passions. In fact, the joy I experience when I indulge my strongest passion is the very experience of my strongest passion proving its strength in the midst of strife.

My weaker passions would put an end to the strife between the different passions coursing through me. My weaker passions would become slaves to my strongest passion, they would be domesticated by my strongest passion so that they would no longer struggle only to be bested. My weaker passions, by yielding to my strongest passion without resistance and living in and for the wake of my strongest passion, would diminish the degree of joy that I experience when I indulge my strongest passion.

My weaker passions want a master and Spinoza tells me to give them a good and proper master. Spinoza in his *Ethics* tells me that my strongest passion, rightly assumed to be my passion for reason, should employ reason to become the most capable domesticator of my weaker passions—this, Spinoza says, is virtue, or self-preservation in accordance with rational perfection.

Fie on Spinozist self-preservation! Ay to Heraclitian self-immolation!

If I would care viciously for my strongest passion, I should not let my strongest passion become the domesticator of my weaker passions. My strongest passion only becomes weaker when it becomes a domesticator, my weaker passions only become even weaker when they become domesticates, and, the diminishment of the strife between my many passions is the diminishment of the highest degree of joy I can experience. Instead, if care viciously for my strongest passion, I should employ reason to develop the strength of my weaker passions so that my weaker passions can better challenge my strongest passion and push my strongest passion to become even stronger. My strongest passion may or may not remain my strongest if I care for it viciously—a weaker passion may very well overtake and become my strongest—but, no matter what, heightening the strife between the different passions coursing through me can and will only ever heighten the highest degree of joy that I can experience.

Philosophy & Villainy:

I experience my highest degree of sadness when I come up against barriers, physiological and/or semiological, to the indulgence of my strongest passion, and these most crushing experiences of sadness are the mothers of my most marvelous inventions.

To overcome physiological barriers to the indulgence of my strongest passion, I will invent new prosthetic devices: new technologies. To overcome semiological barriers to the indulgence of my strongest passion, I will invent new poetic devices: new tropes: new metonyms (a.k.a., new reductions), new metaphors (a.k.a., new perspectives), new ironies (a.k.a., new dramatizations), and new synecdoches (a.k.a., new representations).

I always experience my highest degree of sadness concomitantly with, and in equal measure to, my highest degree of joy—I feel my highest degree of joy insofar as my strongest passion proves itself in the strife between the many different passions coursing through me, but my highest degree of joy is accompanied by my highest degree of sadness insofar as my strongest passion, after overcoming the psychological barriers constituted by my other passions, fails to overcome physiological and/or semiological barriers. Thusly, to the extent that there are physiological and/or semiological barriers to the indulgence of my strongest passion, a diminishment of the highest degree of joy I can experience is also a diminishment the highest degree of sadness I can experience and, vice versa, a heightening of the highest degree of joy I can experience is also a heightening of the highest degree of sadness that I can experience.

There are those who would diminish the highest degree of sadness they can experience and, thus, in equal measure, diminish the highest degree of joy they can experience and their impetus for invention: I call such individuals "the exhausted".

Then, by contrast, there are those who would heighten the highest degree of joy they can experience and, thus, in equal measure, heighten the highest degree of sadness they can experience and their impetus for invention: I call such individuals "exuberants".

Among exuberants, there are those who would willingly erect physiological and/or semiological barriers to the indulgence of their strongest passion in order to arouse their highest degree of sadness and the impetus for marvelous inventions: I call such individuals "transformers".

A philosophical concept is a poetic device invented to overcome a semiological barrier to indulging a passion for reason. Leibniz, a self-deceiving transformer, was a most remarkable creator of philosophical concepts. The poor reader of Leibniz, losing themselves in Leibniz's self-deceptions, will accuse Leibniz of (or praise Leibniz for) erecting so many semiological barriers to indulging passion(s) for reason: they do not realize that, in effect, Leibniz erected these barriers as an impetus for marvelous philosophical inventions.

Deleuze is among the few who have seen through Leibniz's self-deceptions. "Imagine Leibniz," Deleuze entreated his students, "there is something frightening there. He is the philosopher of order, even more, of order and policing, in every sense of the word 'policing.' […] He only thinks in terms of order. But very oddly in this taste for order and to establish this order, he yields to the most insane concept creation that we have ever witnessed in philosophy. Disheveled concepts, the most exuberant concepts, the most disordered, the most complex […] [Leibniz] always need[ed] to have other, always other concepts. One witnesses a mad creation of concepts. […] He never finished creating something new."

Philosophy & Villainy:

Hume scandalizes those who would shamefully adopt the guise of the philosopher honest-man, those who would deny that there is a difference between passion(s) for reason and reasons-in-themselves. "Reason is, and ought only to be the slave of the passions," Hume (in)famously wrote, "and [reason] can never pretend to any other office than to serve and obey [the passions]."

So, reason is the servant of the passions—yes, but what, then, is a passion for reason?

A passion for reason is a passion for serving one's passions, for caring for one's passions, either virtuously (by diminishing the strife between one's different passions) or viciously (by aggravating the strife between one's different passions).

The exhausted philosopher is the philosopher who cares virtuously for their passions; the exuberant philosopher is the philosopher who cares viciously for their passions. Hume teaches us that, although all philosophers are indeed villains, the exhausted philosopher's villainy is the sort of villainy that is commonly taken to be virtuous. Modest degrees of joy and sadness, achieved by diminishing of the strife between one's different passions, are unlikely to offend others and are, thus, commonly considered virtues. Extreme heights of joy and sadness, achieved by aggravating the strife between one's different passions, are very likely to cause offense to others and are, thus, commonly considered vices.

Hume shows us that some devious artifice or contrivance is always at work when an extreme height of joy and sadness is widely considered a virtue in a given society at a given time and place. Through Hume we may come to better appreciate the pretenses of high culture: the devious means by which the ordinary are persuaded and/or seduced to endure the offense of comparing their own lowly joys and sadnesses to the tremendous joys and sadness of the extraordinary. Without such devious pretenses, virtue would otherwise always be coterminous with impoverished joys and sadnesses, with those degrees of joy and sadness that are the least offensive to the lowest common denominator in a given society at a given time and place.

The paths of traditional philosophy (the paths along which we discover ultimate universals) and the paths of defeatist philosophy (the paths along which we discover ultimate transversals) were paths well established by the ancients. The paths of critical philosophy (the paths along which we discover generative universals) were not entirely unknown to the ancients but they were first vigorously explored by the moderns. The early modern rationalists, Descartes, Spinoza, and Leibniz, forged critical philosophical paths that departed from but always connected back to traditional philosophical paths.

Kant was the first assuredly modern philosopher, the first to forge critical philosophical paths that were a definitive break from traditional philosophical paths. Prior to Kant, transformative philosophy was only communicable as a wild departure from defeatism; since Kant, transformative philosophy has also become communicable as a wild departure from criticism.

The defeatist and the transformer are allies in championing transversal concepts over and against universal concepts but they are rivals insofar as the generative transversal concepts of the transformer are opposed to the ultimate transversal concepts of the defeatist. The critic and the transformer are allies in championing generative concepts over and against ultimate concepts but they are rivals insofar as the generative transversal concepts of the transformer are opposed to the generative universal concepts of the critic. Another way of putting all of this: the defeatist and the transformer have homologous concepts of space but disparate concepts of time, while the critic and the transformer have homologous concepts of time but disparate concepts of space.

Kant's critical philosophy promotes a new image of the philosopher honest-man. The lived experience of the traditional philosopher-honest man is nothing but a (mis)representation of the ultimate facts of existence given to us by reason; the critical, as opposed to the traditional, philosopher honest-man does not hold that reason gives us the ultimate facts of existence but, rather, that reason gives us universal laws that govern the ever-changing facts of lived experience. The traditional philosopher sought to demonstrate that the ever-changing facts of lived experience were nothing more than illusions concealing the ultimate facts of existence and, it follows, the traditional philosopher endeavored to do away with illusions in order to bring the ultimate facts of existence to light. The critical philosopher finds that the changing facts of lived experience are more than mere illusions: the changing facts of lived experience are so many truths but they are dis-empowered by the lack of order and regularity among them: so, the critical philosopher endeavors to empower these many truths by employing reason to create order and regularity among them.

The Kantian critical philosopher is an exhausted philosopher. The disordered and irregular facts of my lived experience are but the simulacra of the strife between the different passions coursing through me, and creating order and regularity among the facts of my lived experience is coterminous with diminishing the strife between the passions coursing through me, impoverishing my joys, my sadnesses, and my impetus for invention. What the critical philosopher hails as empowering the facts, I would, as a transformative philosopher, decry as enfeebling the passions.

Transformers who do not create a transformative philosophy for themselves must either become masters of self-flagellation or masters of self-deception. Leibniz, an optimist, was a singular master of self-deception; Kierkegaard, a pessimist, was a singular master of self-flagellation.

Leibniz and Kierkegaard were both exuberant creators of concepts: their respective philosophical practices were transformative. Leibniz's great philosophical texts are letters addressed to given persons and expositions addressed to given publics, and Leibniz was always philosophizing differently to benefit the given person or public to whom he addressed himself. Kierkegaard went even further: not only did Kierkegaard philosophize differently depending upon his audience, Kierkegaard invented different authors and philosophized differently depending upon who he imagined was authoring a work and how he imagined the author would address a given public. In either case, for both Leibniz and Kierkegaard, philosophizing was always philosophizing differently.

Leibniz, the master of self-deception, was able to convince himself that, in spite of the fact that he was always philosophizing differently, he was still a philosopher-honest man. Kierkegaard, the master of self-flagellation, saw himself always in an unforgivable state of sin, always engaged in an absurd search of atonement, always asking God to forgive his interminable and, thus, unforgivable villainy. Kierkegaard's philosophical works present us with so many different demonstrations of the fact that there can only be philosopher villains, that the philosopher-honest man is nothing but a (self-)deception; for Kierkegaard, the fact that none of us can ever truly become a philosopher-honest man is the divine fact of our fundamentally sinful nature. Even if our strongest passion is a passion for God and we put reason in the service of our passion for God, we still sin because we still employ reason as a philosopher villain. Thus, whereas Leibniz's philosophizing always ends with an affirmation of the "pre-established harmony" amongst myriad differences, ensuring that Leibniz is an "honest to God" philosopher, Kierkegaard's philosophizing always ends with Kierkegaard's authors' condemning themselves for their own sinful philosophical villainy.

13. Kierkegaard

A transformative philosophy refuses to strike a happy balance between Leibnizian optimism and Kierkegaardian pessimism. Instead, a transformative philosophy reverses the terms of Leibnizian optimism and Kierkegaardian pessimism. A transformative philosophy is pessimistic where Leibniz's philosophy is optimistic and it is optimistic where Kierkegaard's philosophy is pessimistic: a transformative philosophy is an affirmation of both the absence of a pre-established harmony and the absence of honest-to-God philosophers or, in other words, a transformative philosophy is an affirmation of unceasing strife and the enduring villainy of philosophers.

Philosophy & Villainy:

14. Nietzsche

Transformative philosophy is pre-modern insofar as it is communicable as a wild departure from defeatist philosophy, but it is postmodern insofar as it is communicable as a wild departure from critical philosophy.

Kant, the first assuredly modern-critical philosopher, invites me to increase the overall regularity of the ever-changing facts of my lived experience and, in so doing, maintain my passions in a state of perpetual peace. Nietzsche, the first assuredly postmodern-transformative philosopher, invites me to perpetuate and intensify the strife between the different passions coursing through me and, in so doing, increase the (re-) occurrence of anomalies amongst the ever-changing facts of my lived experience.

Kant's invitation is an invitation to become virtuous in the eyes of the majority; Nietzsche's invitation is an invitation to become vicious in the eyes of the majority. Nietzsche, like Hume, knows full well that virtue is commonly associated with the lowly joys and sadnesses of those whose passions are at peace and that vice is commonly associated with the tremendous joys and sadnesses of those whose passions are at war. Indeed, Nietzsche, even more than Hume, allows me to better appreciate the pretenses of high culture—his *Genealogy of Morals* is all about the devious means by which the ordinary are seduced to endure the offense of comparing their own lowly joys and sadnesses to the tremendous joys and sadnesses of the extraordinary.

Nietzsche, however, does not ask me to hide behind the pretenses of high culture: he only lets me know that the pretenses of high culture are there for me to hide behind when the rule of the majority threatens to overwhelm and crush my body or my spirit. Nietzsche, instead, dares me to be openly exuberant, to endure as much rancor from the majority as I can. My impetus for invention is heightened by the experience of being persecuted by rancorous majorities, just as it is dampened by comfortable living behind the pretenses of high culture. The pretenses of high culture—esteem and authority given to and received from an aristocracy or a meritocracy—enervates more than it enlivens when high culture becomes anything more than a temporary mobile refuge from the rancorous rule of the majority.

(Re)Creative Genius:

1. Embodying Phantasms

Let us say that I have a desire to be *like* Sir David Attenborough. I act on my desire by taking Sir Attenborough as a role model: I seek to produce in myself a group of stereotypical characteristics that I can attribute to Sir Attenborough. Insofar as Sir Attenborough is a famous naturalist and broadcaster, I may strive to become a famous naturalist and broadcaster. — All of this is what you may call the external mediation of my desires by my impressions of Sir Attenborough.

Let's say that I have successfully become like Sir Attenborough: I have reproduced in myself the stereotypical characteristics that I attributed Sir Attenborough: I am now a famous naturalist and broadcaster. Now, let's say that the BBC wants to produce a spectacular new nature documentary and that they are considering hiring Sir Attenborough to narrate the new documentary. The gig as narrator of the next big BBC nature documentary is transformed into a simulacra when my desire to become like Sir Attenborough inspires me to become his rival and to compete with him for this gig. — All of this is what you may call the internal mediation of my desires by my impressions of Sir Attenborough.

Let's say that I get that gig narrating the new BBC documentary and then I get another gig over Sir Attenborough and then another and then another. I now feel that I have bested Sir Attenborough, that he is neither a worthy role model nor a worthy rival. Indeed, Sir Attenborough is revealed to be less than what I had imagined him to be. The figure that I formed from my impressions of Sir Attenborough, the figure that became my role model and then my rival, was nothing but a phantasm. So, I no longer take Sir Attenborough for a role model or a rival but, instead, realize that the Sir David Attenborough I had emulated and rivaled was my phantasm all along and I now openly strive to embody this phantasm, to become everything that I imagined Sir Attenborough to be but now know him not to be. — All of this is what you may call my metaphysical desire to embody my impressions of Sir Attenborough.

(Re)Creative Genius:

Just like filial imprinting birds of a given species may imprint upon creatures of another species and upon non-living forms, the mimetic desires of *Homo sapiens* may be mediated by creatures of other species and by non-living forms. For instance, if my desire is mediated by a bird that I encounter and I take this bird for my role model, I may endeavor to learn how to fly an aeroplane and, thus, produce in myself the bird's most stereotypical characteristic, a capacity for flight. Another example, if my desire is mediated by a mountain that I've seen off in the distance and I take this mountain for my rival, I may endeavor to climb to the peak of this mountain and speak of conquering its height.

The forms of memetic desire described above are most fascinating to me because phantasms are expressed most pronouncedly in our stereotypes and our simulacra when our memetic desires are mediated by entities to which we bear little to no resemblance.

The example involving Sir Attenborough deployed above involved my emulating and rivaling another individual of my own species whom I resemble in many ways. Such scenarios allow me to remain unconscious of my phantasms for as long as I (i) fail emulate my role model and (ii) fail to best them as rival. A consciousness of one's phantasms may arise much, much earlier when one seeks to emulate and rival a being that bears little to no resemblance to oneself. Indeed, one's failure emulate and rival an entity radically different from oneself is not a hindrance to becoming conscious of one's phantasms but, rather, an impetus to become conscious of one's phantasms. One is least likely to become conscious of one's phantasms when one fails to emulate and rival a person that one closely resembles because the differences between oneself and one's role model and rival get lost in resemblances: *one's phantasms are found in the differences between oneself and one's role models and rivals.*

2. Phantastic Role Models & Rivals

Becoming conscious of one's phantasms does not put a stop to the production of stereotypes and the fabrication of simulacra. To the contrary, stereotypes and simulacra proliferate much more wildly when one becomes conscious of one's phantasms and proceeds to embody them. The difference between being conscious of one's phantasms and being unconscious of one's phantasms lies in the fact that everything is reduced to stereotypes and represented by simulacra when one is unconscious of one's phantasms: stereotypes are regarded as synecdoches and simulacra are regarded as metonyms. By contrast, everything becomes irreducible and nothing can be represented when one becomes conscious of one's phantasms: stereotypes become ironies instead of synecdoches, simulacra become metaphors instead of metonyms. In other words, emulating role models and competing with rivals becomes fun and games, a form of (re)creation, when one becomes conscious of one's phantasms; by contrast, one takes role models and rivals seriously, all too seriously, when one is unconscious of one's phantasms.

Those whose role models and rivals are reasonably close to them are those who are slowest to become conscious of their phantasms: for most of their "mature" lives, they are likely to take everything, including fun and games, seriously, far too seriously, and they will not admit the importance of mere nothings. Those whose role models and rivals are phantastically far from them are those who are quickest to become conscious of their phantasms: they are the quickest to see through the façade of maturity, to realize that everything is recreation and nothing should be taken seriously; or, even better, they are the quickest to realize that phantasms, which are mere nothings, are all that should be taken seriously.

(Re)Creative Genius:

Poetry seduces us to take on phantastic role models and rivals. Without poetry many of us are likely to find ourselves caught in the Oedipal triangle, forever emulating and rivaling Mommy or Daddy, and those of us who manage to escape the Oedipal triangle are still likely to emulate and rival similar beings, beings with whom we sympathize. Poetry inspires us to emulate and rival beings that we do not resemble by fostering empathy with these different beings. Poetry teaches us to empathize with the sun, the moon and the stars, the mountains, the desert and the oceans, the atom and the void; and with empathy for different beings comes the impetus to emulate and rival different beings.

Most of us learn to empathize with, emulate and rival radically different beings through original works of poetry. The (re)creative genius, however, is one who empathizes with, emulates, and rivals radically different beings not through original works of poetry but, rather, through their own poetic sensibility: their poetic vision (their sense of sight), their poetic flair (their sense of smell), their poetic gusto (their sense of taste), their poetic feeling (there sense of touch), their poetic ear (their sense of hearing), their poetic verve (the sense for language), their poetic dynamism (their sense of motion), etc. A (re)creative genius creates original works of poetry by emulating and rivaling radically different beings, and these are the original works of poetry that inspire most of us to empathize with, emulate and rival radically different beings.

(Re)creative geniuses are those who become conscious of their own phantasms the fastest, thanks their own poetic sensibility. Those who are not (re)creative geniuses but encounter works of (re)creative genius will become conscious of their own phantasms sooner than they would have if (re)creative genius never appeared. Those who are not (re)creative geniuses and never encounter works of (re)creative genius are slowest to become conscious of their phantasms.

Archetypal Schizoanalysis:

The cliché psychoanalyst successfully "treats" their patients by getting their patients to "traverse" the phantasies that the unwanted symptoms of their mental illnesses represent. In other words, the cliché psychoanalyst guides their patients to recognize the "reality" of their phantasies, the aspects of their phantasies that transcend imagining. The "reality" of every phantasy, according to the cliché psychoanalyst, is an unspoken/unspeakable desire, and a phantasy is successfully traversed by a patient when a patient learns to speak of their unspoken/unspeakable desire—this is why they call psychoanalysis the "talking cure". For most of his career, Freud thought that the unspoken/unspeakable desires of his patients were their desires to break taboos: most profoundly, desires to break the "universal" taboo against incest and patricide. But Freud, during his later years, and Lacan, following Freud, came up with a richer idea of what desires were unspoken/unspeakable. For the late Freud and, after him, Lacan, a patient's unspoken/unspeakable desires were not desires for anything at all but, rather, desires for nothingness, for death and destruction. Desires for death and destruction are often, but not always, expressed as desires and wishes to break taboos because breaking a taboo invites death and destruction. From this perspective, a cliché psychoanalyst treats their patients by getting their patients to speak aloud their desires for death and destruction: the idea being that, when one cannot repress one's desire for death and destruction, speech can discharge this desire in a manner that destroys the speaker virtually rather than actually, a manner that is more or less harmless, that leaves the speaker's actual existence more or less intact as it is.

The schizoanalyst, by contrast, argues that there is no such thing as a desire for death and destruction: desire is always creative or, even better, desire is creativity itself. We only appear to have a desire for death and destruction insofar as we would conserve what has already been created, conserve who we already are. Freud and Lacan were conservatives: they could see their patients as having desires for death and destruction because it was their job to help their patients maintain an existing status quo. Deleuze and Guattari were radicals: they recognized that desires for death and destruction were conservative (mis)representations of desires to (re)create life otherwise, anew. So, rather than traversing our phantasies by speaking aloud our desire for death and destruction, schizoanalysis guides us to (re)create life otherwise, after our phantasies. Now, this does not mean that we should all go fuck our mothers and kill our fathers like Oedipus: no! A desire to break a taboo is only a reification of the destructive aspects of our desire to (re)create life otherwise.

1. Phantastic Desires

Our phantasies are characterized by forms that can be traced back to realities that we despise and wish to destroy, yes, but our phantasies are also characterized by forms that are completely and utterly phantastic, forms that we have never encountered in reality, forms that map paths along which we may (re)create life otherwise. Freud and Lacan cast the imaginary as an an-archic agent of destruction by dismissing unreal, phantastic desires as abstractions and reifying real, taboo desires; Deleuze and Guattari cast the imaginary as an-archic agent of creation by reifying unreal, phantastic desires and dismissing real, taboo desires as abstractions. For Freud and Lacan, the unwanted symptoms of our mental disorders index our failure to repress real, taboo desires, desires for death and destruction; for Deleuze and Guattari, the unwanted symptoms of our mental disorders index our failure to express surreal, phantastic desires, desires to (re)create life otherwise. Freud and Lacan would "treat" us by getting us to use speech to (re)cast desires to (re)create life otherwise as real, taboo desires, as desires for death and destruction. Against Freud and Lacan, not only do Deleuze and Guattari guide us to speak of our phantastic desires to (re)create life otherwise, they also, more importantly, guide our bodies to act on, act out, enact our phantastic desires to (re)create life otherwise.

Jung was, like Deleuze and Guattari, fascinated by surreal, phantastic desires. This is most evident in the manner that Jung differed from Freud in his readings of myths and stories. Freud thought that myths and stories were compelling because they were (mis)representations of real, taboo desires, and they were most compelling when they were (mis)representations of that most real, taboo desire: the desire that I may triumph in the Oedipal love triangle between Mommy, Daddy, and Me. Jung scoffed at this idea. Jung was convinced that myths and stories were compelling because they give us perspectives on our surreal, phantastic desires. Jung argued that the enduring appeal of the most compelling myths and stories had less to do with their appeal to real, taboo desires that are shared by a population and much more to do with surreal, phantastic desires that are shared by a population. "Archetypes" are what Jung called these surreal, phantastic desires that populations shared, and Jung thought that the (re)creation of archetypes was the only means for people to gain a sense and understanding for each other's surreal, phantastic desires. For Jung, only the (re)creation of archetypes enabled communions between the surreal, phantastic desires of different persons, communions able to effect collaborative (re)creations otherwise.

Archetypal Schizoanalysis:

The practice of the cliché psychoanalyst revolves around the following question: "How does a subject effectively represent their own desire as a desire for death and destruction, a desire to break the Oedipal taboo, a desire that they must acknowledge, yes, but only to then disavow?" To understand this question, however, one must first understand that the cliché psychoanalyst believes that one remains an immature, pseudo-subject until one represents one's desire as described above—in other words, the cliché psychoanalyst believes that mental disorders are forms of arrested development that perpetuate forms of pseudo-subjectivity, and every mental disorder is defined by (i) the stage at which a subject's development has been arrested and (ii) the specific impediments that arrest the subject's development.

The cliché psychoanalyst diagnoses an individual with autism when their subjective development is arrested at the intrauterine stage of life. The autistic pseudo-subject hasn't properly been born: they do not recognize that their body is an object apart from the body of their (m)other: they feel as if their body is still part and parcel of their (m)other's body, as if they never left the womb. The autistic pseudo-subject cannot be compelled to speak aloud of their own frustrated desire to couple with their (m)other because they are, affectively and effectively, coupled with their (m)other.

The cliché psychoanalyst diagnoses an individual with psychosis when an individual is "born" and separated from their (m)other objectively but not subjectively. Unlike the autistic pseudo-subject, the psychotic pseudo-subject recognizes that their body is, effectively, an object separate from their (m)other's body, but the psychotic pseudo-subject does not recognize that they are a subject: they are affectively still coupled with their (m)other. The (m)other is the only true subject for the psychotic pseudo-subject, and the psychotic pseudo-subject is itself nothing more than an object that their (m)other may or may not desire. The psychotic never asks, "What do I want?" Instead, the psychotic pseudo-subject asks, "What does my (m)other want?" The psychotic cannot be compelled to speak aloud of their own frustrated desire to couple with their (m)other because they know nothing of their own subjective desire: they only know of their (m)other's desire. The psychotic only speaks of their (m)other's desire for them or their (m)other's desire for another. As such, a paternal figure can only appear to the psychotic pseudo-subject as another object that the (m)other may or may not desire.

2. (M)other Fuckers

The cliché psychoanalyst diagnoses an individual with a borderline personality when an individual is objectively and subjectively born and separated from their (m)other but an individual does recognize that a paternal figure has the authority to prohibit them from coupling with their (m)other. The borderline pseudo-subject, who recognizes their own subjective desire to be the object of the (m)other's desire, treats the paternal figure as a rival, as another subject who wants to be the object of the (m)other's desire. The paternal figure is a figure to be challenged, contested, dueled not a figure to be respected. The borderline pseudo-subject can be compelled to speak aloud of their own frustrated desire to couple with their (m)other, but they cannot be compelled to forswear their desire to couple with their (m)other.

The cliché psychoanalyst diagnoses an individual with a perversion when an individual recognizes the authority of a paternal figure in their speech but not in their actions. A perverse pseudo-subject will claim that they recognize the authority of a paternal figure but, in spite of this, they will still act on their desire to destroy themself by coupling with their (m)other: they will say that they have forsworn their desire to couple with the (m)other but they will do otherwise.

The cliché psychoanalyst wants us to become balanced, mature subjects, to become individuals who acknowledge their desire to couple with their (m)other but recognize and defer to the authorities that prohibit them from coupling with their (m)other.

Archetypal Schizoanalysis:

The practice of the archetypal schizoanalyst operates on five basic assumptions:

1. All the world's a market and all of us mere manufacturers, fabricating organized bodies to fulfill the orders prevailing upon the market.

There are three ways that we may fulfill a prevailing order: *balanced fulfillment* produces sufficient, well-organized bodies, as ordered; *manic fulfillment* exceeds orders, producing over-organized bodies, bodies in surplus, having more than what is sufficient; *depressive fulfillment* disappoints, producing under-organized bodies, bodies that lack, having less than what is necessary. Manic fulfillment and depressive fulfillment are two paths along which one may co-opt and détourn a prevailing order and fulfill one's own singular, idiosyncratic order, one's own desire to (re)create otherwise: the manic-depressive manufacturer fortuitously alternates between exceeding and disappointing prevailing orders: fortuitously playing both sides against the middle so as to fulfill their own singular, idiosyncratic order, their own desire to (re)create otherwise.

2. Those who fulfill their own their own singular, idiosyncratic orders, i.e., those who (re)create otherwise, are disordered relative to prevailing orders.

We have a *depressive affective disorder* when we disappoint a prevailing order and properly signify disappointment by devaluing our bodily organization; a *manic affective disorder* when we exceed a prevailing order and properly signify excitement by valuing our bodily organization highly; a *manic-depressive affective disorder* when we alternate between exceeding and disappointing a prevailing order and properly signify excitement and disappointment accordingly; and *balanced, orderly affects* when we properly fulfill a prevailing order and properly signify contentment assigning a fair value to our product.

We have a *psychotic disorder* when we dissent and values our body according to our own singular, idiosyncratic order: when we properly fulfill a prevailing order and signify disappointment or excitement instead of contentment, undervaluing or overvaluing our balanced bodily organization; when we disappoint a prevailing order and signify excitement or contentment instead of disappointment, either demanding a fair value for or overvaluing our disappointing bodily organization; when we exceed a prevailing order and signify contentment or disappointment instead of excitement, either demanding a fair value for or undervaluing our excessive bodily organization.

3. Every prevailing order effects its fulfillment by affecting an unorganized body—that is to say, every prevailing order effects the organization of a body by affecting a body without organs.

A body without organs is *gladly affected* by prevailing orders that effect manic over-organizations. A body without organs is *badly affected* by prevailing orders that effect depressive under-organizations. A body without organs is *unaffected* by prevailing orders that effect balanced organizations. A body without organs is *fortuitously affected* by prevailing orders that effect manic-depressive organizations, organizations that are by fortuitous turns either manically over-organized or depressively under-organized.

4. A cliché is a prevailing order which leaves a body unaffected.

In other words, a prevailing order is a cliché when it effects a balanced organization of a body. A prevailing order becomes a universal cliché when each and every body is unaffected by it or when rules, norms, and/or protocols effectively outlaw, institutionalize, and/or monitor those bodies that are affected by a prevailing order, be it gladly, badly, or fortuitously.

5. An archetype is a prevailing order which affects a body, be it gladly, badly, or fortuitously.

In other words, a prevailing order is an archetype when it effects a manic and/or a depressive organization of a body. A prevailing order becomes a universal archetype when each and every body is affected by it, either gladly, badly, or fortuitously, or when a rules, norms, and protocols that effectively outlaw, institutionalize, and monitor those bodies that are unaffected by a prevailing order.

Archetypal Schizoanalysis:

4. The Wisdom of Silenus

The archetypal schizoanalyst guides each and every body to insist upon an archetype that fortuitously affects them but without universalizing the archetype, without enforcing/reinforcing rules, norms, and protocols that would effectively outlaw, institutionalize, and monitor those who are (un)affected otherwise. If the archetype that fortuitously affects you is that of Oedipus, so be it, you can and should insist upon it, but, while you insist upon the myth of Oedipus, I, for example, will insist upon the archetype of the Minotaur, which fortuitously affects me.

Insofar as you and I would commune and collaborate with one another, the archetypal schizoanalyst would encourage us to insist upon a syncretic, transversal archetype that passes through both the myth of Oedipus and that of the Minotaur. The archetypal schizoanalyst would find fault with me if I were to outlaw, institutionalize, and/or monitor you for being otherwise (un) affected by the myth of the Minotaur apart from the myth of Oedipus; and the archetypal schizoanalyst would find fault with you if you were to outlaw, institutionalize, and/or monitor me for being otherwise (un)affected by the myth of Oedipus apart from the myth of the Minotaur.

Burlesque, farce, and parody, as opposed to righteous indignation, are the weapons with which the archetypal schizoanalyst combats the cliché psychoanalyst: the archetypal schizoanalyst prefers to play the satyr as opposed to the saint, to play Silenus to others' Dionysus. Cliché psychoanalysts are not to be preached against: they are to be caricatured, lampooned, spoofed, taken to ludicrous tragicomic extremes. Mock them with the wisdom of Silenus, "It is best not to be born at all, to be autistic; and next to that, it is better to court death, to be a proud borderline-psycho-(m)other-fucker, than to live perversely or properly minding your father's rules, norms, and protocols."

Technologies of Self-Parody:

1. Foucault's Arrow

Today, I pick up an arrow, Foucault's arrow, and fire it elsewhere, otherwise, in a different direction.

Following Foucault, I speak of four different "matrices of practical reason": first, that of the technologies of production, "which permit us to produce, transform, or manipulate things"; second, that of the technologies of signification, "which permit us to use signs, meanings, symbols"; third, that of the technologies of domination, "which determine the conduct of individuals and submit them to certain ends"; fourth, and finally, that of the technologies of self, "which permit individuals to effect by their own means or with the help of others a certain number of operations on their own bodies and souls, thoughts, conduct, and way of being, so as to transform themselves".

Following Foucault further, I direct my attention to the last two "matrices of practical reason", those of the technologies of domination and of self, keeping in mind, however, that all four matrices of practical reason inform and interact with one another.

And, finally, following Foucault to the end—that is, the end of his life and career—I do not "insist too much in the technology of domination" but, rather, insist in the technology of self, keeping in mind, again, that the technologies of domination and of self, though different, work in tandem. Indeed, today, I wager that either (i) a technology of domination emerges as a supplement to a technology of self or, vice versa, (ii) that a technology of self emerges as a supplement to a technology of domination.

Foucault, throughout his career, investigated technologies of self but, for the most part, Foucault considered technologies of self as supplements to technologies of domination. At the end of his life and career, however, Foucault made a Copernican turn: investigating the possibility that technologies of domination, prior to being supplemented by technologies of self, emerged first as supplements to technologies of self.

I pick up Foucault's arrow here, as a philosopher not a historian, and, what's more, as a "philosopher villain", one dealing with his own daemons, rather than an "honest-to-God" philosopher.

I leave the archival work to others with the time, the resources, and the temperament for it. Instead, I try my luck, speculate, make wagers, give chance a chance, and dare you to call my bluffs.

Technologies of Self-Parody:

I wager that there are four different technologies of self to be discovered: the technologies of self-mastery, of self-discipline, of self-control, and of self-parody. Let us take these one by one.

First, I find the *technologies of self-mastery.* Consider: the Walkabouts of aboriginal Australians, the ritual lion hunts of the Maasai, the early modern European ritual of the duel, and finally, perhaps the most primal technologies of self-mastery: those rituals surrounding the agonies of nativity that esteem (m)otherhood. What makes each of these technologies of self-mastery? They are all rituals through which one affirm one's sovereignty over one's own body and its passions by making a spectacle of enduring agony and chancing annihilation.

To exhibit a technology of self-mastery for you, what might I do? Instigate a slight resulting in one of you challenging me to a duel: we all step outside, pistols are fired, and, chancing annihilation in front of you all in a ritualized agonistic spectacle, I affirm my sovereignty over my own body and its passions.

Technologies of sovereign domination, sovereign power, were, at first, supplements to technologies of self-mastery: subjugating others' bodies and passions was, at first, a way that one endured agony and chanced annihilation in order to affirm one's sovereignty over one's own body. Somehow, at some point, some complex factors allowed certain technologies of sovereign domination to come into their own and "supplementalize" technologies of self-mastery: others began to submit to a master whether or not a master agonized and chanced annihilation in order to become a master.

Moving on, I find the *technologies of self-discipline*: which make demonstrating one's fitness to oneself a matter of routine exercise. We find technologies of self-discipline in ancient Greece and Rome, among the Stoics and the Epicureans, whose philosophies affirmed forms of routine exercise through which one demonstrated one's fitness to oneself.

To exhibit a technology of self-discipline what might I do? I present the record of my exercise regimen: three days a week, every week, month after month, year after year: swimming so many laps, running so many miles, and oh so many bench presses. That is self-discipline, no?

2. Mastery, Discipline, Control

During the European Enlightenment, technologies of disciplinary domination, disciplinary power, came into their own and "supplementalized" technologies of self-discipline Subjugating others' bodies became a matter of subjecting others to routine examinations: compelling others to demonstrate their fitness on demand at certain intervals, and confining and correcting those examined and found unfit.

Third, I find the *technologies of self-control*: making self-maintenance and self-sustenance a matter of protocol, emerging when individuals begin asking "How do I maintain and sustain the fitness that I routinely demonstrate?" Or, in other words, as an Epicurean might put it, "How do I care for myself?"

To exhibit a technology of self-control what might I do? Self-discipline, the routine demonstration of one's fitness, can damage the self if one is not careful. I break my arm, for instance, but keep performing the same exercises three days a week, every week, my arm won't heal properly: my self-discipline will wreck my body: I demonstrate self-discipline without self-control. Self-control means modulating in a self-maintaining, self-sustaining manner: dialing down or dialing up routine exercises according to some protocol in order to maintain and sustain a certain measure of fitness as a statistical result.

Technologies of controlling domination solve the problem of sustaining and maintaining social discipline without wrecking a society. Technologies of controlling domination come into their own and supplementalize technologies of self-control and when measures of social well-being (a certain birth rate, crime rate, graduation rate, rate of morbidity, rate of economic growth) are maintained and sustained as statistical results over durations of time, and no longer regarded as demands to be met at given points in time.

Technologies of Self-Parody:

Finally, there are the *technologies of self-parody*. Technologies of self-parody cannot propagate apart from the other three technologies of self. Self-mastery, self-discipline, and self-control are constructive, they construct the self; by contrast, self-parody is deconstructive, it deconstructs the self. The deconstructive infects and alters the constructive like a virus infects and alters a host. Self-parody does not negate self-mastery, self-discipline, or self-control: self-parody co-opts self-mastery, self-discipline, and self-control, like a virus co-opts its host.

The cynicism of Diogenes was a technology of self-parody that played with self-mastery. The cynic laughs, "Feral dogs, those creatures said to be most in need of a master, are, ironically, caricatures of all who want self-mastery. Those wanting self-mastery resent and loathe their own doggishness: they want self-mastery in order to minimize their own doggishness. Watch as I make a mockery of those who want self-mastery: watch as I maximize my own doggishness by co-opting technologies of self-mastery."

The libertinism of Sade was a technology of self-parody that played with self-discipline. The libertine laughs, "Outrageous voluptuaries, those very personages said to lack self-discipline the most, are, ironically, caricatures of all those who want self-discipline. Those wanting self-discipline resent and loathe their own voluptuosity: they want self-discipline in order to minimize their own voluptuosity. Watch as I make a mockery of those who want self-discipline: watch as I maximize my own voluptuosity by co-opting technologies of self-discipline."

Today, I present a technology that plays with self-control: I co-opt, pervert, and subvert the technology of psychotherapy, in particular the technology of psychoanalysis: the *pater familias* of psychotherapy, who, like King Lear, laments the wickedness of its heirs from a position of infirmity.

Regard, Freud's steam engine model of the mind. Our Ids produce flows of phantasies that fuel our Super-Egos to produce a greater or lesser sense of reality. Too great a sense of reality, too few phantasies fueling our Super-Egos, and we become psychotics. Too slight a sense of reality, too many phantasies fueling our Super-Egos, and we become neurotics. Our Egos are escape valves that maintain an optimal sense of reality by either expressing and reducing the phantasies fed to our Super-Egos or repressing and increasing the phantasies fed to our Super-Egos.

3. Cynics, Libertines, Schizophrenics

The psychotic mind wants self-control either (i) because, in catatonic cases, its Id does not produce enough phantasies to sustain and maintain an optimal sense reality or (ii) because, in paranoid cases, its Ego does not repress enough phantasies to sustain and maintain an optimal sense reality. By contrast, the neurotic mind wants self-control because its Id produces phantasies in excess but its Ego does not express enough phantasies to sustain and maintain an optimal sense of reality.

The psychoanalyst services minds that want an optimal sense of reality, minds with Egos that do not express and repress phantasies in a self-sustaining and self-maintaining manner—minds wanting self-control.

My "archetypal schizoanalysis", the technology of self-parody that I present to you today, ridicules any and all notions of an "optimal sense of reality" and, instead, affirms an Ego that fortuitously modulates the expression and repression of phantasies to no end, without intents and purposes. The archetypal schizoanalyst is kin to the mad scientists of steampunk: less interested in optimizing the workings of the engine and more interested in maximizing the engine's ability to work and fail, to function and malfunction, fortuitously, and in so many different ways.

Schizophrenics, those with fortuitously (dis)ordered senses of reality, are, ironically, caricatures of all those who want self-control. Those wanting self-control resent and loathe the fact that their existence is entropic, noisy, fortuitous: they want self-control in order to minimize the entropy, noise, and fortuity that mars their existence. Let us mock those who want self-control: let us maximize the entropy, noise, and fortuity that mars our existence by co-opting the technologies of self-control.

Emmanuelle's Cunt:

Cynic. Libertine. Anarchist. — If I am either to be misjudged or to be judged and found wanting, I shall betray nothing by courting these judgments: either judge me a cynic, libertine, and anarchist or judge me for wanting to be judged a cynic, libertine, and anarchist.

As a *cynic*, I wager that I am always slave to my strongest passion, for to master one passion is to be enslaved by another, stronger passion. If I have mastered my passion for sex, for instance, such that I may eschew all sexual activity, it is because I am a slave to another, stronger passion: my passion for reason. If I refuse to indulge my passion for sex it is only because my passion for reason, which is itself a carnal passion, runs counter to my passion for sex—my passion for sex, if it is to be indulged, must either put itself in the service of my strongest passion, my passion for reason, or it must ally with other, weaker passions with whose help it may overpower my passion for reason.

As *libertine*, I wager that all forms of ascetic self-discipline are, in fact, forms of hedonistic self-indulgence. If a person meditates for an hour a day, day after day, week after week, month after month, year after year, I say that it is because that person gets hot, gets wet, and gets off on meditation. Self-discipline does not mean keeping to routines in spite of one's passions but, rather, keeping to routines that indulge one's passions. All self-discipline is self-indulgence: if I lack self-discipline it is because I have not yet discovered routines that indulge my passions.

As *anarchist*, I wager that the most optimal distribution of events is the most random distribution of events: the distribution with maximum entropy and maximum dispersion. Those who fight against entropy aim to achieve an average of, say, twenty-five orgasms a month by creating a non-uniform distribution of events, for instance, by creating a "normal distribution" of events—by coming as close as they can to having twenty-five orgasms every month, so that, on any given month, they will most likely have had twenty-five orgasms and it will be most unlikely that they will have had the minimum possible, zero orgasms, or that they will have reached their record maximum of, say, fifty orgasms. The anarchist, by contrast, is unpredictable: the anarchist aims for a maximally dispersed, uniform distribution of events: I may have twenty-five orgasms a month on average, but on any given month it will be equally likely that I will have my minimum, zero orgasms, my record maximum, fifty orgasms, or any number of orgasms in between zero and fifty.

As anarchist, I do not eschew targeting a certain mean or desiring a certain average, but, rather, I eschew arriving at a targeted mean or a desired average by minimizing entropy and dispersion; as anarchist, I endeavor to arrive at a targeted mean or a desired average by maximizing entropy and dispersion.

Emmanuelle's Cunt, a novel that I shall never be finished writing, is the story of the making of a cynic, libertine, and anarchist, the story of my own making: an autobiography, yes, but a factless autobiography, a fabulated autobiography. I have a prick, Emmanuelle has a cunt, and the differences between Emmanuelle and I only start there, yet, that being said, Emmanuelle and I are so alike in our differences, we dissimulate one another so well that we shall forever confound all those who endeavor to tell us apart.

Hypocrite readers, — *my dissemblers,* — *my accomplices!* — I am, and I shall always and forever be, becoming—a cynic, libertine, and anarchist in the making. As the story of my making has no end, the writing of *Emmanuelle's Cunt* will never come to an end, will come without end.   So, in lieu of a finished novel, a novel which will never come, I offer you what has come so far, in fits and spurts. Make of this spunk what you will.

Emmanuelle's Cunt:

The *Farce of Pure Pussy* is a journey through hell: Emmanuelle's *Inferno*. I am tempted to write the farce in lines terza rima:

Gully. Gorge. A pit to be probed. A chasm.
  — Iconography of the urinal? Or
  Pussy's purest, noumenal being? His vim
hollows Hers, floods, fills to the brim; and (M)others
  gender *d'Autres*, Sires, and Sons; and Daddy's
  Girls whet Momma's Boys for a Father's pleasure,
fascinate—their valleys, fecund, uncanny
  Depths, unplumbed—the measures of Man, awaited.
  Phallacies! — Sham Oedipal fictions damming
up strange wantings coursing beyond us; fated
  forms, of hatreds born, of resentments issued,
  fix the err to gender desire, bait the
taboo. *Pussy* — purely and simply — tissues,
  matter, forces — foldings of flesh — *an organ*,
  not a body, rather, a part, a bit loosed
from a whole: a likeness, at best, of its sum.
  Bodies: wholes — not things-in-themselves — *for-themselves*,
  rather, *no-things*. Pussy as void, as chasm:
part mistaken, taken for difference itself.

Too obscure? Perhaps... Instead, let me begin with an epigraph, a choice passage from the "Polemical Preface" to Angela Carter's *The Sadeian Woman*:

Anatomy is destiny, said Freud, which is true enough as far as it goes, but ambiguous. My anatomy is only part of an infinitely complex organization: my self. The anatomical reductionalism of graffiti, the reductio ad absurdum of the bodily differences between men and women, extracts all the evidence of me from myself and leaves behind only a single aspect of my life as a mammal. It enlarges this aspect, simplifies it and then presents it as the most significant aspect of my entire humanity. This is true of all mythologising of sexuality; but graffiti lets it be seen to be true.

1. The Farce of Pure Pussy (Inferno)

Ay! That is pure pussy, no? Pussy as the "ultimate universal" fact of woman's existence: pussy de-historicised, de-worlded, removed from sensuous experience—pussy mythologized by the reactionary poet or, even worse, theorized by the reactionary philosopher. *Pure pussy! Fie!* —Carter, again, "We may believe we fuck stripped of social artifice; in bed, we even feel we touch the bedrock of human nature itself. But we are deceived. Flesh is not a human universal."

If I were writing the *Critique of Pure Pussy*, I would counter Carter and demonstrate that, while Flesh is not an "ultimate universal" fact of human existence, Flesh is a "generative universal" schema that regulates the facts of human existence—but this is *Emmanuelle's Cunt*, not Immanuel Kant. I am writing the *Farce of Pure Pussy*: I side with Carter and treat Flesh as a "generative transversal" phantasy dissembling and disseminating so many anarchic, counter-factual passions.

The *Farce of Pure Pussy* follows Emmanuelle, my alter-ego, my Rrose Sélavy, as she fucks her way through hell—through the reactionary's "ultimate universal" facts of Flesh, through the critic's "generative universal" schemas of Flesh, and through the killjoys "ultimate transversal" betrayals of Flesh—discovering, in and through all this fucking, Flesh as "generative transversal" phantasy.

Emmanuelle's Cunt:

Emmanuelle's Cunt poses the following questions — "Who to fuck, when, where, how, with what appendages and orifices, and why?"

The reactionary, the partisan of ultimate universal facts, is one who seeks to terminate all lines of questioning with unequivocal, totalizing answers—which is to say, the reactionary seeks to put everyone and everything in their proper place and make sure that everyone and everything stays settled in their proper place. In seeking answers to the questions posed by *Emmanuelle's Cunt*, the reactionary is, at bottom, seeking an answer to the following question, "How do I put Emmanuelle's cunt in its proper place and keep it there?"

The critic, the partisan of generative universal schemas, is one who seeks to initiate all lines of questioning with unequivocal, totalizing answers—which is to say, the critic seeks to circumscribe the travel and settlement of everyone and everything by assigning everyone and everything a proper channel of communication and transportation. In seeking answers to the questions posed by *Emmanuelle's Cunt*, the critic is, at bottom, seeking an answer to the following question, "How do I steer Emmanuelle's cunt away from certain fucks and towards other fucks for right and proper reasons and along right and proper paths?"

The killjoy, the partisan of ultimate transversal betrayals, is one who seeks to terminate all lines of questioning with equivocal, shifting answers—which is to say, the killjoy gives everyone and everything the freedom to travel anyplace while denying them the freedom to settle anyplace. In seeking answers to the questions posed by *Emmanuelle's Cunt*, the killjoy is, at bottom, seeking an answer to the following question, "How do I ensure that Emmanuelle's cunt keeps going from one fuck to another and never has a chance to linger in love?"

The anarchist, the partisan of generative transversal phantasies, seeks to initiate all lines of questioning with equivocal, shifting answers—which is to say, the anarchist seeks to give everyone and everything the freedom to travel to anyplace and settle anyplace along fortuitously disordered paths. In seeking answers to the questions posed by *Emmanuelle's Cunt*, the anarchist is, at bottom, seeking an answer to the following question, "How can I rouse Emmanuelle's cunt to try its luck differently, to speculate, to make wagers, to give chance a chance, to take random walks along fortuitously disordered paths, to go from one fuck to another and to linger in love according to serendipity?"

1. The Farce of Pure Pussy, cont'd

Carter: "The notion of the universality of human experience is a confidence trick and the notion of the universality of female experience a clever confidence trick."

Agreed.

It follows that the reactionaries, with their ultimate universal facts of human experience, and the critics, with their generative universal schemas of human experience, both belong in the eighth circle of Hell, the *Malebolge*, reserved for those who commit "honest frauds" against Flesh.

The killjoys, with their ultimate transversal betrayals, belong in the ninth and lowest circle of Hell, the *Cocytus*, reserved for those who commit "treacherous frauds" against Flesh.

I will dispense with the other seven circles of hell, for all other crimes against Flesh are afterbirths of honest and/or treacherous frauds. — The *Farce of Pure Pussy* follows Emmanuelle as she fucks her way through a series filthy gutters (the *Malebolge*), through arcs of bitter lamentations (the *Cocytus*), down Satan's back and into *Purgatory*, into the *Farce of Practical Pussy*.

Emmanuelle's Cunt:

1. The Farce of Pure Pussy, cont'd

A PLAN OF EMMANUELLE'S
JOURNEY THROUGH HELL

Gutter 1:
Emmanuelle fucks Broad Shoulders [Plato]

Gutter 2:
Emmanuelle fucks the Handyman [The Stoic]

Gutter 3:
Emmanuelle fucks the Gardener [The Epicurean]

Gutter 4:
Emmanuelle fucks the Fangirl [The Epic Poet]

Gutter 5:
Emmanuelle fucks the Football Team [The Spartans]

Gutter 6:
Emmanuelle fucks the Sisters of St. Francis [The Pious]

Gutter 7:
Emmanuelle fucks the Perfectionist [Spinoza]

Gutter 8:
Emmanuelle fucks the Maestro [Leibniz]

Gutter 9:
 Emmanuelle fucks the Jurist [Kant]

Gutter 10:
Emmanuelle fucks the Social Justice Warriors [the Marxists]

Lamentation 1:
Emmanuelle's laments the conceptualization of Pussy.

Lamentation 2:
Emmanuelle laments the (mis)representation of Pussy.

Lamentation 3:
Emmanuelle laments the (dis)simulation of Pussy.

Lamentation 4:
Emmanuelle laments the iconography of Pussy.

Satan's Backside:
Emmanuelle laments the indexing of Pussy.

Emmanuelle's Cunt:

Yet one more effort cosmopolitans if you would become cynics, libertines, anarchists!

Moralists do not teach us to master our passions, rather, they teach us to lie to others and to ourselves about the passions that have mastered us, the passions we are slave to. Moralists teach us to point to vicious passions that have been tamed and to claim that they have been conquered by virtue when, in fact, they have only been conquered by other vicious passions. — I say that I have mastered my gluttonous passions and learned the virtue of moderation when I refuse a second slice of cake but, in fact, I have become slave to vain passions that have grown stronger than my gluttonous passions.

Would that we were taught to mind the vicious passions that constitute us, to consider under what conditions this vice can vanquish that vice, and these other vices form alliances, and those other vices mutually assure each other's defeat! Instead, culture gives us "morality lessons": we are taught to turn away from our vices and to make a pretense of either wanting virtue or having attained virtue. Let us counter culture! Where moralists find virtue and vice, let us find one vice conquering and flagellating another— what moralists call virtues are conquering vices, and what moralists admit to being vices are conquered vices.

For instance, if I "recognize" that my lust is a vice it is because my lust has run afoul of some other vice(s), say, my avarice and my pride, which have allied to overpower my lust, if only for a moment. Having overpowered my lust for a time, my avarice and my pride flagellate my lust and I find myself thinking, "Fie on lust! I would have money and self-esteem if I hadn't been a slave to my lust, if my lust hadn't motivated me to spare no expense and eschew no degradation for the pleasures of Flesh." Whenever we find ourselves condemning one of our vices, we must ask ourselves, "*Cui bono?* Which of my other vices benefits from my condemning this vice?" I condemn my sloth when indulging my pride demands that my home epitomizes cleanliness. I condemn my pride when it keeps me from taking the easy money and indulging my avarice and sloth.

As a cynic, I do not turn away from my vices, even now. I know full well that I am indulging vicious passions in this very writing. I admit, I envy those who are able to fool themselves into thinking that they want or have attained virtue and, because I cannot fool myself into thinking that I want or have attained virtue, I endeavor to spoil things for others, to keep others from fooling themselves in ways that I cannot. What's more, my envy recovers my pride: not only do I get to spoil things for those who have fooled themselves, I get to feel pride in the fact that I have not fooled myself. Yes, my cynicism is the triumphant alliance of my envy and my pride.

2. The Farce of Practical Pussy

The Ends. —To create conditions that would allow us to indulge each and every one of our vices—our avarice, our profligacy, our sloth, our gluttony, our lust, our pride, our wrath, etc.—and to indulge each and every one of our vices in such a way that we are not inclined to make a pretense of virtue that condemns any of one our vices.

The Means. —To create anarchy—to maximize the entropy and dispersal that characterizes the distribution of our indulgences. We shall have achieved our ends when we achieve a maximally dispersed, uniform distribution of indulgences, when, at any given moment, the likelihood that we will indulge any one vice is the equal to the likelihood that we will indulge any other vice.

We do not need to create one single, elaborately regimented, meticulously timed, and implacably disciplined macro-routine that would allow us to indulge all of our vices simultaneously or in succession, a la Sade's *120 Days of Sodom*. Indeed, if the totalitarian libertinism of Sade's *120 Days of Sodom* is Wagnerian Gesamtkunstwerk, our anarchistic libertinism is an aleatoricism. Why emulate the tediums of the Château de Silling when we may, instead, create serendipity, create conditions that foil attempts to render affinities and enmities between our vices predictable, so that no single vice and no coalition of vices can reliably benefit from condemning any other single vice or coalition of vices.

Ay! Let us create so many different and disparate micro-routines that indulge so many different and disparate vices and let us create protocols to select amongst these micro-routines at random and in such a way that maximizes the entropy and dispersal that characterizes the distribution of our indulgences. Let us free ourselves of virtue by indulging vice serendipitously.

Emmanuelle's Cunt:

.

A PLAN OF EMMANUELLE'S
JOURNEY THROUGH PURGATORY

Terrace 1:   Trophy Pussy
[Emmanuelle fucks with pride]

Terrace 2:   O. P. P.
[Emmanuelle fucks with jealousy.]

Terrace 3:   A Dish Best Served Cold
[Emmanuelle fucks with vengeance.]

Terrace 4:   Pussy Will Provide
[Emmanuelle fucks with lassitude.]

Terrace 5:   Assets and Expenditures
[Emmanuelle fucks with greed.]

Terrace 6:   An All You Can Eat Buffet
[Emmanuelle is a glutton for fucking.]

Terrace 7:   Pussy! Pussy! Pussy!
[Emmanuelle can't help giving a fuck.]

Emmanuelle's Cunt:

TO KNOW ONESELF

To make a self-righteous pretense of virtue, to claim that one either wants or has attained a virtue, to fatally betrays one's vices to oneself and to others in and through one's self-righteous pretension—this is what is I call a *becoming un-conscious of one's vices.*

To make a farce of wanting and attaining virtue, to vitally betrays one's vices to oneself and to others in and through farce—this is what is I call a *becoming conscious of one's vices.*

TO LOVE

To seek and endure deep and sustained intimacy with another person when one is unconscious of one's own vices: to sustain an unconscious wish that you and your other could make a farce of virtue together—this is what is I call *double-blind, fatal love.*

To seek and endure deep and sustained intimacy with another person who appears unconscious of their vices when one is conscious of one's own vices: to persist in making a farce of virtue in front of your other, when your other is either unconscious of their vices or averse to betraying their vices to you—this is what is I call *single-blind, fatal love.*

To seek and endure deep and sustained intimacy with another person who is conscious of their vices when one is also conscious of one's own vices, to make an enduring farce of virtue with your other—this is what is I call *discerning, vital love.*

3. The Farce of the Power of Cunt

TO LUST

To seek and endure only a shallow and fleeting intimacy with another person when one is unconscious of one's own vices and, thus, cannot discern whether or not the other is conscious of theirs—this is what is I call a *double-blind, fatal attraction*.

To seek and endure only a shallow and fleeting intimacy with another person who appears unconscious of their vices when one is conscious of one's own vices—this is what is I call a *single-blind, fatal attraction*.

To seek and endure only a shallow and fleeting intimacy with another person who is conscious of their vices when one is also conscious of one's own vices—this is what is I call a *discerning, vital attraction*.

TO MAKE ONESELF SCARCE

To avoid intimacy with another person when one is unconscious of one's own vices and, thus, cannot discern whether or not the other is conscious of theirs—this is what is I call a *double-blind, vital aversion*.

To avoid intimacy with another person who appears unconscious of their vices when one is conscious of one's own vices—this is what is I call a *single-blind, vital aversion*.

To avoid intimacy with another person who is conscious of their vices when one is also conscious of one's own vices—this is what is I call a *discerning, vital aversion*.

Emmanuelle's Cunt:

TO LIVE & LOVE JOYFULLY

Aversion is the greater part of life in a (post)modern metropolis. Going to work, being at work, running errands, passing through any kind public setting, real or virtual—everywhere we go we must repel and be repelled by so many gazes from and brushes with strangers and we must elude and escape so much small talk with so many beings unconscious of their vices. These aversions are vital and we should learn to enjoy them! To return so many gazes, so many touches, so many conventional calls and responses—to accept so many invitations to be guilted, pitied, and brutalized for one's vices—what could be more fatal! To flee the fatal, to elude and escape death a thousand times in a single day—what could be more vital!

Amidst so many aversions, however, we do experience a few minor attractions: we are struck by the bearing and style of a passing stranger and we invite the stranger to momentarily exchange glances, brush-up against us, and make small talk. Some of these minor attractions are mutual, some are not. If you invite a stranger to momentarily exchange looks and the stranger averts their eyes, recognize that your invitation is fatal and that their aversion is vital: to pester them with further invitations, to pester them in spite of their aversion, such a choice is as fatal to you as it is to them because, even if a minor attraction is mutual, a minor attraction remains fatal when it won't develop into a major attraction.

A major attraction is an escalating procession of reciprocated minor attractions resulting in a degree of intimacy that affords a reciprocal exchange of vital betrayals. A reciprocal exchange of vital betrayals can only take place when the parties to a mutual attraction collaborate to fabricate a *mise-en-scène* that makes a farce of virtue and, depending upon the *mise-en-scène* involved, such collaborations demand a greater or lesser degree of intimacy between parties to a mutual attraction. That being said, even if a sufficient degree of intimacy is achieved, there can be no reciprocal exchange of vital betrayals if any of the parties involved are unconscious of their vices. Major attractions can only be vital when they involve individuals who are already conscious of their vices, who are willing and able to vitally betray their vices to one another; major attractions that do not lead reciprocal exchanges of vital betrayals will remain fatal unless they develop into love.

Love is an escalating procession of major attractions resulting in a degree of intimacy that allows individuals to become conscious of their vices with and through one another: quantity becomes quality, with a sheer magnitude of accumulated fatal betrayals one can piece together a vital betrayal, but it is like piecing together a four dimensional pointillist picture puzzle whose completed image has never been seen before and whose puzzling pieces endlessly proliferate.

3. The Farce of the Power of Cunt, cont'd

Love remains fatal until the pointillist picture puzzles are pieced together, until each lover becomes conscious of their own vices, in and through one another, and they collude to make a farce of virtue together. Alas, we who are conscious of our vices realize that the only sort of relationships worth having with those who are unconscious of their vices are loving relationships. As the vast majority are unconscious of their vices, and as the vast majority of attractions will never develop into love, we who are conscious of our vices are averse to the vast majority. What's more, because love is a grueling endeavor, we who are conscious of our vices only endeavor to love when a fatal attraction is convulsive: fatal attractions that aren't attended by convulsions aren't worth pursuing.

We who would embody our vices are so few and far between and there is no superficial characteristic that enables us to easily pick each other out from a crowd. Indeed, we can only recognize one another other for what we are after an escalating procession of reciprocated minor attractions develops into a major attraction, affording us an opportunity reciprocally exchange vital betrayals.

Knowing full well how fatal it is for us to consummate most minor attractions, we who would embody our vices will eschew all minor attractions that aren't convulsive. That being the case, however, convulsive minor attractions are not assuredly those that involve others who would embody their vices: more often than not, we are convulsively attracted to others who are unconscious of their vices. No matter, however, the point is this: if we who would embody our vices are to find one another, we must make ourselves convulsively attractive and charming, and this is the *Farce of the Power of Cunt*, joyful living in Emmanuelle's *Paradiso*: to devote one's life to making oneself convulsively attractive and charming, yes, but enigmatically so—so as to elude and escape the approaches of those who are unconscious of their vices.

A joyful life is a life spent cultivating an obscure glamour, arousing and gratifying the vices of joyful others, others who embody their vices, while distancing oneself from dismal others, others who make a pretense of wanting or attaining virtue. To love joyfully is to help those you love cultivate an obscure glamour, to help those you love arouse and gratify the vices of joyful others, yourself amongst them, and to help those you love ward off the self-righteous pretension of dismal others.

Libidinal Economics:

1. Custom, Profit, and (Re)Creation

The *customary use* of a knife may be to assist with eating, with hunting, with carving, or with a ceremonial bloodletting ritual—whatever the case may be, a knife fabricated and apprehended with a customary use in mind is an object fabricated and apprehended as a *fetish*, as a constant good.

By contrast, the *profitable use* of a knife is either (i) to be exchanged for another good or (ii) to be employed in the production of another good to-be-exchanged—but, in either case, a knife fabricated and apprehended with a profitable use in mind is an good fabricated and apprehended as a cliché or formulaic good or, in other words, fabricated and apprehended as a form of *capital*: as commodity-capital when the knife is itself exchanged for another object, as productive capital when the knife is used to produce and transport another object that is to-be-exchanged, as money capital when the knife is used as currency for so many different exchanges of goods.

In our (post-)industrial societies customary uses are supplementary to profitable uses: an ever increasing number of objects are fabricated and apprehended not with a specific customary use in mind but, rather, with a profitable use in mind, and, what's more, purely customary uses—that is, customary uses that are not supplementary to profitable uses—are frowned upon for being "unproductive".

There is another sort of "unproductive" use, however, a sort that may be supplementary to profitable use without being customary: the (re)creative use of goods in the research and development of profitable uses, in the prototyping of profitable uses. The *(re)creative use* of a knife, for instance, is the unprofitable, non-customary use of a knife in the prototyping of profitable uses, and a knife fabricated and apprehended with a (re)creative use in mind is fabricated and apprehended as a prototypical good or, in other words, as a *probe*.

Libidinal Economics:

Small societies that revolve around the familiarity of their members and the simple manufacture of goods are societies that pay little mind to the difference between the production of goods and the customary uses of goods. The larger and more complicated a society and its manufacturing processes become, the more unfamiliar the consumers of goods are to producers of goods, and the more profitable uses come to mediate between the production of goods and their customary uses. In other words, an individual who will not have a familiar experience with the customary use of a good will not participate in a good's production unless participation in a good's production is profitable to them. If I make a dress for my wife, I need not make any profit from the making of the dress because I get to experience the customary use of the dress alongside my wife when she wears it. The factory workers in the Philippines who make a dress that Emmanuelle will buy and wear to a house party in Brooklyn will want to profit from the labor that they put into the dress because they will not share the experience of the customary use of the dress.

The larger societies become, the more complicated their manufacturing processes become, the more unfamiliar consumers of goods are to producers of goods, the more profitable uses mediate between the production of goods and the customary uses of goods—but also, the more (re)creative uses come to precede profitable uses. When I make a dress for my wife, I know her customary activities and I tailor the dress to her customary activities. If I am the dressmaker in a small town, I may not experience all of my customers' uses of my products, but I shall have a fairly good feeling for what those uses are and I can tailor my dresses for those uses so as to ensure that my goods meet a demand. If I am manufacturing dresses that will be sold to strangers all around the world, I will need to tailor my product to different markets that I must research and I shall need to develop prototypes and test the appeal of my prototypes in different markets so as to gauge or, better still, stimulate demand for my product.

Customary uses are primary and all other uses are supplementary in pre-capitalist societies and in societies that react against capitalism.

Profitable uses are primary and all other uses are supplementary in the (post-)industrial capitalist societies that prevail in our day and age.

I would like you to dream with me, if you will, of a post-capitalist future where (re)creative uses are primary and all other uses are supplementary.

In spite of the preceding genealogy, it would be a mistake to treat customary uses as if they preceded profitable and (re)creative uses. Indeed, to the contrary, I say that (re)creative use is the initial or larval stage of use, that profitable use is the pupal stage that follows, and that customary use is the imago or the mature form of use.

Capitalist societies are regressive rather than progressive: they arrest the maturation of most uses at the profitable, pupal stage. My post-capitalist future is even more regressive than the capitalist present: I dream of a future in which most uses languish in the (re) creative, larval stage. Pre-capitalist societies and societies that react against capitalism are the most progressive societies, they insist that most uses mature into customary uses.

In small scale pre-capitalist societies, the larval-(re)creative and pupal-profitable stages of use are accelerated to such a degree that they have no prominence: the imago-customary stage of use accounts for the greater part of use, while the larval-(re)creative and pupal-profitable stages are of lesser account. As societies grow and their manufacturing processes become more complex: first the pupal-profitable stage is prolonged and gains prominence, then the larval-(re)creative stage is prolonged and gains prominence, and, all the while, imagos or customary uses gradually lose prominence.

Capitalist societies are societies in which the pupal-profitable stage accounts for the greater part of use, while the larval-(re)creative and imago-customary stages of use are of lesser account. Capitalists promote growth and complexity, yes, but only up to a point, up to the tipping point at which the larval-(re)creative stage of use threatens to become more prominent than pupal-profitable stage.

The larval-(re)creative stage of use accounts for the greater part of use in my post-capitalist future, and it follows that, in order to arrest the development of uses earlier than capitalist societies do, my post-capitalist future demands larger and more complex societies and manufacturing processes than those of capitalist societies.

Libidinal Economics:

A customary use is a use according to an assumed *code*. Knives are coded for cutting, books are coded for reading, and sex is coded for reproduction: custom would code a use for a thing then use a thing accordingly.

A profitable use assumes no code as its own but, instead, assumes a *protocol* for translating between codes. In fact, a profitable use is, itself, a translation according to an assumed protocol. Knives can be exchanged for books, books exchanged for sex, sex exchanged for knives, and money is a protocol that facilitates such exchanges.

A (re)creative use assumes neither a code nor a protocol as its own. A (re)creative use is a *measure* of (un)translatability, a measure of whether and to what degree translation is achievable under different conditions. (Re)creative uses ask and answer the following questions — Is there money to be made is the sale of knifes, or books, or sex? If so, in the sale of what sorts of knives, books, or sex? When, where, and how do knives, books, or sex gain currency, lose currency, become currency? And, in a given time and place, who forms the market for knives, for books, for sex? — Note, however, that to act on established answers to these questions would be to make profitable uses of knives, books, and sex; (re)creative uses of knives, books, and sex only ask these question and search for different answers to these questions.

Reactionary anti-capitalists (the partisans of customary uses) are "on the money", so to speak, when they accuse capitalists (the partisans of profitable uses) of lacking a moral or ethical code of their own. But if capitalists are deplorable for having no code of their own, just how much more deplorable are experimentalists (the partisans of (re)creative uses)? Don't capitalists come nearer to having a code of their own than experimentalists do?

What is coded via customary use, contractualized via profitable use, and measured via (re)creative use? The (un)translatability of our desires; or, in other words, the (in)communicability of our desires.

I make (re)creative use of my body by endeavoring to answer the following question, "When, where, how, and for whom does my body gain currency, lose currency, become currency?" In so doing, I measure whether, to what degree, and under what conditions my body can communicate others' desires.

I make profitable use of my body by either exchanging it as currency or exchanging it for currency. Either way, in so doing, I contractualize the conditions under which my body communicates others' desires—or, in other words, I follow a protocol that specifies certain conditions under which my body communicates others' desires.

My wife makes customary use of my body, she makes love to my body, and, in so doing, my body becomes code for my wife's desire to make love—or, in other words, the communication of my wife's desire to make love becomes conditional upon my body.

Libidinal Economics:

To live is to make use of one's body; to live amongst others is to let others make use of one's body and to make use of others' bodies. An ethics orders us to make use of our own bodies in some fashion or other, and a politics orders us to make use of others' bodies and let others make use of our bodies in some fashion or other.

Reactionary anti-capitalists, the partisans of customary uses of bodies, do not eschew (re)creative and profitable uses but, rather, consider (re)creative and profitable uses to be "necessary evils" that precede customary uses but are not be tolerated once customary uses have been established. In other words, reactionary anti-capitalists insist that communicable desires are coded and, once communicable desires have their coded customary uses, reactionary anti-capitalists endeavor to put a stop to (re)creative and productive uses. (Re)creative and profitable uses of bodies that lead to the establishment of customary uses are "necessary evils", but (re)creative and profitable uses that do not establish customary uses are "pure, unnecessary evils" and their partisans are "evil doers". The ethics and politics of reactionary anti-capitalists are about either punishing or forgiving "evil doers".

Capitalists, the partisans of profitable uses of bodies, do not eschew (re)creative and customary uses but, rather, consider (re)creative and customary uses to be losses that bracket profitable uses and, while losses are to be minimized, some losses are, alas, inevitable. In other words, capitalists insist that communicable desires are contractualized and, once communicable desires have been contractualized, capitalists endeavor to mitigate losses resulting from customary and (re)creative uses in breach of contract. (Re) creative and customary uses of bodies that bracket profitable uses in some manner, shape, or form are "rational investments", but (re) creative and customary uses that do not bracket profitable uses are "irrational investments" and their partisans are "irrational actors". The ethics and politics of capitalists are all about damage control: bad investments and irrational actors are unfortunate facts of life that must be controlled for, and the capitalist or "rational actor" must learn to cope with bad investments made by irrational actors.

Experimentalists, the partisans of (re)creative uses, do not eschew profitable and customary uses but, rather, consider profitable and customary uses to be sources of measurement errors. Random errors in measurements, which are the results of customary uses, are unavoidable but can be accounted for. Systematic errors in measurements, which are the results of profitable uses, can be rejected, corrected, and trivialized. Repeated (re)creative uses achieve measurements of greater and greater precision insofar as the random errors of customary use are accounted for in the distribution of so many repeated measurements. Varied (re)creative uses achieve measurements of greater and greater accuracy insofar as the systematic errors of profitable uses can be rejected, corrected, and trivialized by superpositioning distributions of so many varied measurements to achieve, in sum, a maximally dispersed and maximally entropic distribution.

To account for random error by repeating experiments is to engage in the *dismal (re)creative use* of bodies; to reject, correct, and trivialize systematic errors by varying experiments, is to engage in the *gay (re)creative use* of bodies. Gay (re)creative uses, however, are nothing apart from dismal (re)creative uses: *gay (re)creative uses are ~~dismal (re) creative uses~~*.

Libidinal Economics:

5. Allies, Partners, Co-Investigators

Reactionary anti-capitalists seek *customary alliances*: they seek to be of customary use to others and to make customary use of others. I go golfing with Jill, go skiing with Jack, and have sex with Dorothy: Jill, Jack, and Dorothy are customary allies of mine, each one is of customary use to me and I am of customary use to them.

Capitalists seek *business partnerships*: they seek to be of profitable use to others and to make profitable use of others. I go golfing with Jill and I go skiing with Jack and, in exchange, I gain social currency: I make profitable use of Jill and Jack. Dorothy has sex with me and, in exchange, Dorothy gets paid: Dorothy makes profitable use of me. Dorothy accompanies me on a golfing outing with Jill and on a skiing outing with Jack: Dorothy gets paid for the outing and meets new clients, I gain social currency and I get discount on Dorothy's services: Dorothy and I make profitable use of each other, we are business partners.

Experimentalists seek *co-investigators*: they seek to be of (re)creative use to others and to make (re)creative use of others. I wonder how I may gain currency, lose currency, or become currency with and/or for others. Dorothy wonders how she may gain currency, lose currency, or become currency with and/or for others. Neither Dorothy nor I wonder in order to guarantee profitable uses in future: we would just as much gain currency as we would lose currency. Dorothy and I wonder in order to wonder: we experiment both to gain and to lose, in order to learn under what conditions we gain and we lose. I go skiing with Jack instead of Jill and I lose currency; I go golfing with Jill instead of Jack and I gain currency; I have sex with Jack and I gain currency with Jill; I have sex with Jill and I lose currency with Jack. Dorothy paints me instead of having sex with me and she gains currency with me; Dorothy has sex with Jack instead of me and she loses currency with me; Dorothy paints Jill and she becomes currency for both Jack and I, loses currency with Jill, and gains currency with and for herself. I share the methods and results of all my experiments with Dorothy and my experiments come to inspire and inform Dorothy's own experiments. Dorothy shares the methods and results of her experiments with me and Dorothy's experiments come to inspire and inform my own experiments. What's more, Dorothy and I experiment together, wondering how we gain currency, lose currency, or become currency in conjunction with one another: Dorothy and I are co-investigators.

Improbable Aberrations

& Other Idiocies

Force

Just as the finest dancers play with and against physical gravity and fly in spite of physical laws, the finest philosophers play with and against moral gravity and fly in spite of moral laws.

And when the finest dancers are heavy-footed, they are not effectively so, rather, their heavy-footedness is affected. Likewise, the graveness of the finest philosophers is affected.

To maximize my potential, my power to act, my active forces—this, to me, means becoming most light-footed and lighthearted, as fine a dancer and as fine a philosopher as I can become.

Aye! I intend to maximize my potential, and, henceforth, my every word and gesture shall not only announce this intention, again and again, but also index the degree to which I have effected my intention.

So, regard this as an attempt to make light of grave sufferings, to affect them rather than effect them, and, I implore you, judge me and find me wanting if I do not motivate you to live and laugh otherwise, estranged from life's cruelties.

Spirit

To exercise my body like the finest of dancers, to exercise my mind like the finest of philosophers—yes, and more: *to exorcise my spirit like the finest of actors!*

Seek above, below, and beyond the simulacra organizing my body and the stereotypes ordering my mind, and you shall find spirits—daemons disorganizing my body and disordering my mind: phantasms betrayed by my mind in discrete parts, in metonymic bits, and betrayed by my body in continuous waves, in holistic metaphors.

The finest dancers are light-footed and the finest philosophers are lighthearted but the finest actors are, themselves, lights: spirits or daemons exorcised partially in philosophy, wholly in dance, and singularly in drama's juxtaposition of parts and wholes, *rôles* and *mise en scènes*.

Possession, Exorcism, Exhaustion

Evil spirits do not possess and corrupt our bodies and minds. To the contrary, our spirits are possessed and corrupted when we are heavy-footed and heavyhearted, when we hesitate and shrink from maximizing our potential, when our bodies are inactive and our minds reactive

To possess spirits: to be ruled, confined, controlled by my inactive body or my reactive mind.

To exorcise spirits: to be unruly, unconfined, uncontrollable—to actively disorganize my body and disorder my mind, to exercise my body and my mind so as to maximize my potentials and exorcise my spirits.

In so far as my potentials are my potentials and different from yours, the exercises that maximize my potentials and exorcise my spirits will be different from those that maximize your potentials and exorcise your spirits. I must discover the rites and rituals, the mental and physical exercises, the words and gestures that call out my daemons by their names, in their singularly, and you must do the same for yours. Two different individuals cannot share the same rites and rituals of exorcism, they can only inspire and inform each other's different rites and rituals.

An exhausted spirit is a spirit that can no longer be exorcised because it is possessed by a body that is terminally inactive or a mind that is terminally reactive, possessed by a body or a mind that can no longer be affected, a body that can no longer be exorcised.

Physicians, Metaphysicians, Ecstaticians

To exuberantly act as my own physician, to devise and prescribe physical exercises that would disorganize my body and lighten my step!

Exhausting physicians, who treat different bodies likewise, aim to effect good and bad body images: to effect signs of health or illness, of beauty or ugliness.

Exuberant physicians, who treat different bodies otherwise, aim to effect ecstatic paroxysms in themselves and others: to effect convulsions that signify their being beyond health and illness, beyond beauty and ugliness—convulsions that affect health and illness, beauty and ugliness.

To exuberantly act as my own metaphysician, to devise and prescribe mental exercises that would disorder my mind and lighten my heart.

Exhausting metaphysicians, who treat different minds likewise, aim to effect good and bad consciences: to effect signs of virtue or vice, of reason or unreason.

Exuberant metaphysicians, who treat different minds otherwise, aim to effect ecstatic epiphanies in themselves and others: to effect conceptions that signify their being beyond virtue and vice, beyond reason and unreason—conceptions that affect virtue and vice, reason and unreason.

To exuberantly act as my own ecstatician, to devise and prescribe a course of mental and physical exercises, a series of words and gestures, a passage of rites and rituals that would exorcise my spirit.

Exhausting ecstaticians possess good and bad spirits likewise: personifying signs of health or illness, beauty or ugliness, virtue or vice, reason or unreason.

Exuberant ecstaticians exorcise different spirits otherwise, effecting ecstasies in themselves and others, partially through epiphanies, wholly through paroxysms, and singularly through juxtapositions of epiphanies and paroxysms. In other words, exuberant ecstaticians personify signs of their being beyond health and illness, beyond beauty and ugliness, beyond virtue and vice, beyond reason and unreason.

Love

To have exuberant partners to dance with, to live alongside others in whom I would effect greater and greater paroxysms and who would, in turn, effect greater and greater paroxysms in me—or, in other words, to transpire, exchange breaths, with other exuberant physicians: others who would treat their own bodies in ways that inspire and are inspired by my own treatment of my body.

To have exuberant partners to dialogue with, to live alongside others in whom I would effect greater and greater epiphanies and who would, in turn, effect greater and greater epiphanies in me—or, in other words, to transform, exchange information, with other exuberant metaphysicians: others who would treat their own minds in ways that inform and are informed by my own treatment of my mind.

To have exuberant partners to make scenes and to role-play with, to live alongside others in whom I would effect greater and greater ecstasies and who would, in turn, effect greater and greater ecstasies in me—or, in other words, to transpire and transform alongside other exuberant ecstaticians whose paroxysms would inform my epiphanies and whose epiphanies would inform by my paroxysms, whose epiphanies would inspire me to paroxysm and who would be inspired to paroxysm by my epiphanies.

To exuberantly dance and dialogue on my own, with and by myself, in solitude, to bring myself to paroxysm, to prompt my own epiphanies, and to personify my own ecstasies, my own being beyond beings, my being otherwise.

Loathing

To dance with exhausting partners, partners ruled, confined, or controlled by the inactivity of their bodies, by their good or bad body images—partners who cannot see beyond the signs of health or illness, beauty or ugliness that they detect and project

To dialogue with exhausting partners, partners ruled, confined, or controlled by the reactivity of their minds, by their good or bad consciences—partners who cannot see beyond the signs of virtue or vice, reason or unreason that they detect and project.

To make scenes and role-play with exhausting partners, partners ruled, confined, or controlled by inactive bodies and reactive minds, possessing good or bad spirits alike—partners who personify the signs of health or illness, beauty or ugliness, virtue or vice, reason or unreason that they detect and project.

To dance and dialogue myself to exhaustion: to weigh down my spirit with a body image or a conscience, to internalize rules, confines, and controls.

Body and Mind

Paroxyms are happenings that access passions, more or less viscerally; to laugh, to cry, to come—to spasm with a passion.

Epiphanies are musings that (de)note passions, more or less vividly; to put passions into aphorisms or verses.

Ecsstasies are stagings that (re)create (de)noted passions in spasms and (de)note passions (re)created in spasms; to re-access and re-note passions, more or less differently than they have been accessed and noted before.

To have a body image—to make a fetish of my own and others' bodies: e.g., to make a show of the hue and heft my phallus, to fixate upon your callipygian appeal, to curse a genetic defect.

To make myself body without organs—not to be without a body image, without a fetish, but, rather, to be beyond any and all body images, beyond fetishes.

Let fetishes become farcical props, ornaments that affect body images through effective paroxysms: e.g., the hue and heft of a phallus can be affected by a king-sized cuban cigar effectively puffed, your callipygian display affected by a bustle effectively swiveled, the "correction" of a cursed gene for, say, shortsightedness affected by a pair of spectacles effectively sported.

To have a conscience—to (mis)judge and be (mis)judged, to address and redress grievances: e.g., to accuse you of failing to return my love, to make amends for my failure to return your love, to blame my upbringing for making me what I am, to appeal to a higher power for justice or mercy.

To have done with judgment—not to be without any judgment, without conscience, but, rather, to be beyond any and all judgments, beyond conscience.

Let grievances become jokes, philosophical musings that affect judgments through effective epiphanies: e.g., an unrequited lover's lament can be affected by an aphorism that effectively signifies and solicits love, an accusation of neglect can be affected by a verse that effectively signifies and solicits care, the indignity of having to appeal to hierarchy can be affected by a pun that effectively signifies and solicits anarchy.

Cruelties, Estrangements, Immediacies

To be ruled by my body image or by my conscience: to let my body image or my conscience proscribe an exercise of my body or my mind.

To compromise the rule of my body image or my conscience: to circumscribe a rule proscribing an exercise of my body or my mind by carving out so many exceptions to the rule, such that the rule becomes exceptional and exceptions becomes the rule.

To be confined by my body image or by my conscience: to let my body image or my conscience ascribe a limit to my body or my mind.

To riddle the confines of my body image or my conscience: to make a limit ascribed to my body or mind permeable by riddling the boundaries between what is within and what is beyond the limit.

To be controlled by my body image or my conscience: to devise and prescribe for myself exercises geared toward repairing my bad conscience and bad body image or geared towards sustaining my good conscience and good body image.

To lose control: to prescribe so many improvisations: exercises in spontaneity that fortuitously lead to good or bad body images, to good or bad consciences.

Cruelties are exercises that maximize my physical potential by compromising physical rules, riddling physical confines, and letting my body spiral out of control. *Prosthetic devices* are physical rules, confines, and controls that have become indexes of cruelty. Every physical rule that I compromise, every physical confine that I riddle, and every occasion that I lose control of my body indexes the degree to which I have maximized my physical potential.

Estrangements are exercises that maximize my metaphysical potential by compromising metaphysical rules, riddling metaphysical confines, and letting my mind spiral out of control. *Poetic devices* are metaphysical rules, confines, and controls that have become indexes of estrangement. Every metaphysical rule that I compromise, every metaphysical confine that I riddle, and every occasion that I lose control of my mind indexes the degree to which I have maximized my metaphysical potential.

Immediacies are exercises that exorcise my spirit by juxtaposing cruelties and estrangements: by juxtaposing compromised physical and metaphysical rules, juxtaposing riddled physical and metaphysical confines, and juxtaposing bodies and minds spiraling out of control. *Theatrical devices* are physical rules, confines, and controls juxtaposed with metaphysical rules, confines, and controls which together become indexes of immediacy. Every cruelty that informs an estrangement and every estrangement that inspires a cruelty indexes the degree to which I have exorcised my spirit.

Improbable Aberrations:

> *[…] There is, it seems to us,*
> *At best, only a limited value*
> *In the knowledge derived from experience.*
> *The knowledge imposes a pattern, and falsifies,*
> *For the pattern is new in every moment*
> *And every moment is a new and shocking*
> *Valuation of all we have been. […]*
> —T.S. Eliot, "East Coker" from *Four Quartets*

When I write as I am wont to—employing neologisms and puns, irony and humor, enigmas and paradoxes, extremely dense and incredibly terse prose—I do so out of concern for what concerns me.

Writing clearly and plainly is, for me, a frustrating exercise, for to write clearly and plainly about what concerns me is to write without concern for what concerns me. Why am I engaged in such a frustrating exercise now? Can writing a text that is unconcerned with what concerns me persuade others to concern themselves with what concerns me? I doubt it but I will not let doubt deter me from essaying the question: I am desperate to win the concern of others and I know of no better way to win others' concern.

So, you ask, 'What concerns me?'

Well, f(r)iends, what concerns me is the question of *how one lets* **improbable aberrations** *speak and write for themselves.* Aye, and it is my hope that, after reading this text, you will understand that to speak and write clearly and plainly about improbable aberrations is to keep improbable aberrations from speaking and writing for themselves and, if you understand this and you come to share my concern, you won't want me to speak and write clearly and plainly on the subject of improbable aberrations ever again: instead, you will want neologisms and puns, irony and humor, enigmas and paradoxes, extremely dense and incredibly terse prose.

1. What Concerns Me?

So, please do ask the logical next question, 'What is an improbable aberration and why should one let an improbable aberration speak and write for itself?'

Ay! That is *the* question I hope to answer for you with this essay, but I can only begin to answer that question by asking and answering the following question, 'What makes an improbable aberration?' — For an improbable aberration *is* what makes it and, what's more, an improbable aberration should be allowed to speak and write for itself *because* of what makes it. — This sounds awfully *knotty*, I know, but I assure you that I am not trying to be evasive: I am writing as clearly and plainly as I can about the subject at hand. *Bear with me!*

So, I entreat you: indulge me further by asking the following question, 'What makes an improbable aberration?'

I offer this answer, 'Heterogenetic, ontogenetic, and phylogenetic processes that fall out of sync with one another make improbable aberrations.' — I know, I know: I have offered up strange words made stranger by strange usage. Please, I beg you: don't fret! I will explain what I mean, clearly and plainly. *Bear with me and I shall bare all!*

Improbable Aberrations:

2. Heterogeny, Ontogeny, Phylogeny

Phylogenetic processes are processes of grouping, processes that categorize or group existing individuals together to form species, classes, races, nations, tribes, personas and other 'identities'. An example of a phylogenetic process: the process by which a number of individual life forms are grouped together to form a species, like ours, *Homo sapiens*, each individual life form becoming, through this process, a specimen of a species. Species do not pre-exist individuals, rather, species result from the 'sampling' of populations of individuals. Phylogenetic processes are processes that 'sample' populations of individuals, turning individuals into constituents of a category or group, as in my example above, where a phylogenetic process turns individual life forms into specimens of a species. *Phylogenetic processes feed on **onto**genetic processes*—that is to say, phylogenetic processes produce categories or groupings of individuals by processing individuals that have been produced by ontogenetic processes.

Ontogenetic processes are processes of individuation, processes whereby indeterminate potentials are actualized in determinate ways so as to bring individuals into existence. An example of an ontogenetic process: the process by which an individual life form develops auto-poetically, actualizing indeterminate potentials— i.e., the affordances of their genetics and their environment—in a more or less determinate way. Another example: the process by which conducting an experiment with light actualizes, in a more or less determinate way, the indeterminate potential for light to manifest itself as either a wave or a particle, producing individual instances of light being wave and/or individual instances of light being a particle. All this to say that individual beings should not be taken for granted as they are: they are only what they are because they are not what they could be otherwise. Indeed, ontogenetic processes are processes whereby individuals become what they are rather than what they could be otherwise. *Ontogenetic processes feed on **hetero**genetic processes*—that is to say, ontogenetic processes produce individuals by processing affordances that have been produced by heterogenetic processes.

Heterogenetic processes are processes of potentiation, processes that create affordances. Affordances are "pre-individual" potentials, potentials for there to be, or not to be, individuals. Heterogenetic processes are auto-cannibalistic and an-archic, they feed on themselves, processing the very affordances that they produce so as to produce other affordances in an utterly unpredictable manner: one cannot predict whether a heterogenetic process will produce a potential 'to be' or a potential 'not be' and, what's more, there is no way to find out whether the product of a heterogenetic process, a succeeding potential 'to be' or 'not be', was produced via the processing of a preceding potential 'to be' or a preceding potential 'not to be'.

137

Improbable Aberrations:

The *synchrony of* **hetero***genetic and* **onto***genetic processes* produces *probable individuals*. When a heterogenetic process creates a potential 'to be', a concordant potential, and this concordant potential, 'to be', is taken up by an ontogenetic process, an individual resulting from an ontogenetic process is a probable result. Take the example of an experiment with light that actualizes, in a more or less determinate way, the indeterminate potential for light to manifest itself as either a wave or a particle. No matter whether such an experiment takes up light's potential 'to be a wave' or, alternatively, light's potential 'to be a particle': the individual results of any experiment that takes up light's potential 'to be' in any determinate way will be probable: more or less predictable, more or less expected.

The *a*synchrony *of* **hetero***genetic and* **onto***genetic processes* produces *improbable individuals*. When a heterogenetic process creates a potential 'not to be', a discordant potential, and this discordant potential, 'not to be', is taken up by an ontogenetic process, an individual resulting from an ontogenetic process is an improbable result. Keeping with the example above, when an experiment takes up light's potential 'not to be' in any determinate way— that is, light's potential to be neither wave nor particle but, rather, *otherwise than being* a wave or a particle—the individual results of an experiment will be improbable: utterly unpredictable, utterly unexpected.

The *synchrony of* **onto***genetic and* **phylo***genetic processes* produces *gregarious specimens* of a category or group. A gregarious specimen is by definition a probable individual because *a synchrony of* **hetero***genetic and* **onto***genetic processes is a necessary condition for there to be a synchrony of* **onto***genetic and* **phylo***genetic processes.* When ontogenetic processes produce probable individuals that share a likeness and this likeness is taken up by a phylogenetic process, these probable individuals that share a likeness become gregarious specimens of a category or group. Keeping with the example of an experiment with light discussed above, some results among the probable results of such an experiment are more likely results than others, and a practical application of such an experiment, an application that takes up some of the more likely results of such an experiment and puts their likelihood to practical use, is a phylogenetic process that categorizes or groups the results of such an experiment together according to their usefulness, some results being more useful than others, and the more useful results being, in my terms, the more gregarious results.

2. (A)synchronies

The *asynchrony of ontogenetic and phylogenetic processes* produces aberrations, *aberrant specimens* of a category or group. When ontogenetic processes produce individuals that are unlike one another and this unlikeness is taken up by a phylogenetic process, these unlike individuals become aberrant specimens of a category or group. Continuing with the example of practical applications categorizing experimental results according to their usefulness: the more *use**less*** a result is found to be, the less gregarious a result is found to be and the more of an aberration a result is found to be. An aberration may be a probable individual or it may be an improbable individual: a synchrony of heterogenetic and ontogenetic processes is a necessary condition for there to be a synchrony of ontogenetic and phylogenetic processes, yes, but not a sufficient condition—in other words, *there may be synchrony of **hetero**genetic and **onto**genetic processes without their being a synchrony of **onto**genetic and **phylo**genetic processes.*

Probable aberrations, probable individuals that phylogenetic processes construe as aberrations, are only ever *relative aberrations*: although they do not share the likeness that constitutes gregarious specimens produced by a given phylogenetic process, probable aberrations may share other likenesses with one another. In other words, two probable aberrations produced by a given phylogenetic process may share a likeness with one another apart from their being unlike gregarious specimens produced by a given phylogenetic process. By contrast, no two ***im**probable aberrations* produced by a given phylogenetic process will never share a likeness with one another apart from their being unlike gregarious specimens and unlike probable aberrations. In other words, improbable aberrations, improbable individuals that phylogenetic processes construe as aberrations, are always and forever *absolute aberrations*: every improbable aberration is not only *un*like the gregarious specimens produced by a given phylogenetic process but also *un*like any and every other aberration produced by a given phylogenetic process. Returning to the example of the practical applications of an experiment with light, probable aberrations would be relatively useless experimental results, useless only in relation to practical applications that are already given: new practical applications may be forthcoming that could make them useful. Improbable aberrations, by contrast, would be absolutely useless experimental results, useless in relation to any and all practical applications, past, present, and future.

Improbable Aberrations:

So, there you have it, I say improbable aberrations are ~~beings~~ made by heterogenetic, ontogenetic, and phylogenetic processes that have fallen out of sync with one another, and I say we should let improbable aberrations speak and write for themselves because they are made by heterogenetic, ontogenetic, and phylogenetic processes that have fallen out of sync with one another. — There you have it, yes, but I get the feeling that you don't quite have it yet. You've probably got an inkling of what an improbable aberration is, but you're struggling to understand what it means to let an improbable aberration speak and write, for itself or for anything else.

So, please do ask me, 'What do you mean—"to speak and write"— and how does improbable aberration speak and write for itself?'

First, an admission: I have been using the terms 'speaking' and 'writing' figuratively—that is to say, more precisely, synecdochally. Speaking and writing are, for me, exemplary expressions of mimetic desire, and *speaking and writing **for oneself*** is, for me, the most exemplary expression of mimetic desire, which I define as the desire to treat one like another and, in so doing, to constitute a category or group of individuals that are more or less alike. Indeed, speaking and writing are, for me, exemplary expressions of mimetic desire b*ecause every expression of mimetic desire is structured like a use of language and every use of language is an expression of mimetic desire*: every expression of mimetic desire and, thus, every use of language treats one individual like another and, in so doing, constitutes a category or group of individuals that are more or less alike. Ay! Linguistic statements and all other expressions of mimetic desire *never* refer to individuals as such (i.e., to ontogenetic processes and their products). To the contrary, linguistic statements and all other expressions of mimetic desire *always* refer to categories or groupings of individuals (i.e., to phylogenetic processes and their products).

So, what happens when one speaks and writes for oneself? Well, a self is not one individual but, rather, a number of different individuals grouped into an identity, an 'I' or an 'ego'. In this way, a self is itself an expression of mimetic desire—that is to say, an expression of a desire that treats one individual like another individual and, in so doing, constitutes a category or group of individuals. Indeed, *when one speaks and writes about oneself one is actually constructing one's self through a phylogenetic process*, grouping together, into an 'I', of so many different individuals produced by the ontogenetic processes that are one's myriad impulses.

3. The Individual vs. the Self

Some of the individuals that are grouped together to form an 'I' will be gregarious specimens of an 'I'. But many more of the individuals that form an 'I' will be aberrant specimens of an 'I'. 'Gregarious specimens of me' are those versions of me that emerge when my impulses are 'in-sync' with my mimetic desire, when the ontogeny of my self is 'in-sync' with the phylogeny of my self. 'Aberrant specimens of me' are those versions of me that emerge when my impulses are 'out-of-sync' with my mimetic desire, when the *onto*geny of my self is 'out-of-sync' with the *phylo*geny of my self.

Amongst the aberrant specimens of my self, there are what you may call 'probable versions of me' and 'improbable versions of me.' 'Probable versions of me' are those versions of me that emerge when my impulses are 'in-sync' with my fortunes, when the *onto*geny of my self is 'in-sync' with the *hetero*geny of my self. 'Improbable versions of me' are those versions of me that emerge when my impulses are 'out-of-sync' with my fortunes, when the *onto*geny of my self is 'out-of-sync' with the *hetero*geny of my self.

When I say the word 'I', the 'I' that I refer to, *the subject of the statement*, is not any single individual but, rather, a category or grouping of individuals considered together as a unit. By contrast, as opposed to the subject of the statement, *the subject of the enunciation*—that is to say, the subject that enunciates the 'I'—is always an individual, one of the individuals belonging to the category or grouping, 'I'. The subject of the enunciation, the individual, can never refer to themselves as an individual using language: by saying 'I' they can only ever refer to a category or grouping of individuals to which they belong. That being said, however, although the subject of the statement is always the category or grouping of individuals, the subject of the enunciation is always an individual—that is to say, although the individual can never be spoken of or written about, the individual is always the one that speaks and writes, that has and expresses mimetic desire.

But which individual constituent of the category or the group, 'I', is empowered to express their mimetic desire and enunciate the 'I', speaking and writing for the category or group? Is the subject of the enunciation, the enunciator of the 'I', a gregarious specimen of the 'I' or is the subject of the enunciation an aberrant specimen of the 'I'? If the enunciator of the 'I' is an aberrant specimen, is the enunciator a probable aberration or an improbable aberration? To answer these questions, I hypothesize that one must discern the rhythm of a statement, the appeal of statement. While the subject of the statement is always the category or the group as opposed to the individual, the rhythm and appeal of the statement is always that of the individual, the subject of the enunciation.

Improbable Aberrations:

If a statement is *monorhythmic*—appealing to good sense—a statement has been enunciated by a gregarious specimen of the category or group that is the subject of the statement.

If a statement is *polyrhythmic*—appealing to common sense—a statement has been enunciated by a probable aberration with respect to the category or the group that is the subject of the statement.

If a statement is *idiorhythmic*—appealing to nonsense—a statement has been enunciated by an improbable aberration with respect to the category or the group that is the subject of the statement.

Accepting all of the above, it follows that I do not to speak and write about any improbable aberrations individually here in this text but, rather, I speak and write about a category or group consisting of improbable aberrations. All categories and groups are founded upon likenesses amongst individuals, yes, but the likeness that constitutes a category or group of improbable aberrations is a strange, paradoxical likeness: *improbable aberrations are only alike in their being unlike anything and everything else.* Improbable aberrations never share a *positive likeness* with one another: improbable aberrations do not resemble one another nor anyone nor anything else in any way, shape, or form—much to the contrary, each and every improbable aberration can be said to resemble nothing. In resembling nothing, however, each and every improbable aberrations shares a *negative likeness* with one another: improbable aberrations do not resemble one another but they do dissemble one another thanks to their shared resemblance to nothing.

Categories and groupings of individuals that only include improbable aberrations are *idiorhythmic categories* and groupings: when improbable aberrations are the only constituents of a given category or group, only improbable aberrations can speak and write for such a category or group and, thus, all statements about such a category or a group will be idiorhythmic statements, appeals to nonsense.

To let improbable aberrations speak and write for themselves is to let improbable aberrations speak and write of idiorhythmic categories and groupings, to let them express their desire to be treated like what they are, like improbable aberrations.

An expression of mimetic desire is *satisfying* when two or more individuals that have been treated like one another are found to share a positive likeness, a mutual resemblance to someone or something else, and each individual is considered a gregarious specimen, representative of a category or group. In this way, a satisfying expression of mimetic desire is always structured like a monorhythmic statement.

4. Idiorhythmy, Frustration, Ecstasy

An expression of mimetic desire is *ecstasy* when two or more individuals have been treated like one another are found to share a negative likeness, a mutual resemblance to no one and nothing else, and each individual is considered an improbable aberration, constitutive of an idiorhythmic category or grouping. In this way, an ecstatic expression of mimetic desire is always structured like an idiorhythmic statement.

An expression of mimetic desire is *frustrating* when two or more individuals have been treated like one another are found to share neither a positive likeness nor a negative likeness, and one or more of the individuals are considered to be an aberration relative to the others, relative to gregarious specimens of a category or grouping. A frustrating expression of mimetic desire may be structured like a monorhythmic, a polyrhythmic, or an idiorhythmic statement.

The speech and writing of improbable aberrations never satisfies: it is frustrating when improbable aberrations speak and write for gregarious specimens and for probable aberrations; it is ecstasy when improbable aberrations speak and write for other improbable aberrations. That being said, however, one can never predict for whom or what an improbable aberration will speak and write: to let an improbable aberration speak and write is to invite frustration as much as ecstasy: one improbable aberration cannot recognize themself or any other improbable aberration as an improbable aberration until one improbable aberration has tried to speak and write for another and found ecstasy thereby. *Ecstasy being the only sure proof of idiorhythmy, the champion of improbable aberrations must roll the dice, again and again, letting isolated aberrations speak and write, always uncertain as to whether such aberrations are improbable, enduring frustration in pursuit of ecstasy.*

To write clearly and plainly is to write either monorhythmically or polyrhythmically, to appeal either to good sense or to common sense, to either let gregarities write or let probable aberrations write. Aye, and to write clearly and plainly about *im*probable aberrations is to let either gregarities or probable aberrations write about *im*probable aberrations. The writings of gregarities and probable aberrations on the topic of improbable aberrations are, by definition, frustrating expressions of mimetic desire and, what's more, such writings, by definition, are not actually themselves writings on the topic of *im*probable aberrations but, rather, writings on the topic of categories or groups of individuals that include *im*probable aberrations. You will no doubt have noticed that, whenever I wrote about improbable aberrations themselves as an idiorhythmic category or grouping, I failed write clearly and plainly: I had resort to neologisms and puns, irony and humor, enigmas and paradoxes, extremely dense and incredibly terse prose.

So, this was a frustrating exercise, just as I expected, but a worthwhile exercise nonetheless, for I have written a text that dramatizes what it is unable to describe, a text that is performative wherever it fails to be informative or demonstrative.

Performance Notes:

1. What is a Book of Philosophy?

To say that a book of philosophy contains a philosophy is like saying that the score of Beethoven's Große Fuge contains Beethoven's Große Fuge or that the text of Shakespeare's *King Lear* contains the play. Beethoven's Große Fuge is more than its score, Shakespeare's *King Lear* is more than its text. What is the score of the Große Fuge without performances of the Große Fuge? What is the text of *King Lear* without performances of King Lear? The score of the Große Fuge and the text of King Lear are first and foremost notes that enable one to (re)create performances of the Große Fuge and *King Lear*. Similarly, in so far as a philosophy is a singular way of living and knowing, a philosophical text is little more than a set of notes that enable one to (re)create performances of a philosophy, to (re)create a singular way of living and knowing.

Musical scores, dramatic texts, and books of philosophy only contain "certain ciphers on paper." Indeed, Peter Brook's remarks regarding dramatic texts are worth quoting at length here:

Shakespeare's words are records of the words that he wanted to be spoken, words issuing as sounds from people's mouths, with pitch, pause, rhythm and gesture as part of their meaning. A word does not start as a word—it is an end product which begins as an impulse, stimulated by attitude and behaviour which dictate the need for expression. This process occurs inside the dramatist; it is repeated inside the actor. Both may only be conscious of the words, but both for the author and then for the actor the word is a small visible portion of a gigantic unseen formation. Some writers attempt to nail down their meaning and intentions in stage directions and explanations, yet we cannot help being struck by the fact that the best dramatists explain themselves the least. They recognize that further indications will most probably be useless. They recognize that the only way to find the true path to the speaking of a word is through a process that parallels the original creative one. This can neither be bypassed nor simplified.

A philosopher's words are records of concepts that a philosopher wants to be both lived and known, to be both embodied and minded. Aye, and the best philosophers also explain themselves the least.

Performance Notes:

2. Playing Shamelessly

Despite the fact that they are working from more or less the same dramatic text, Ian McKellen's becoming-Lear was different from Glenda Jackson's becoming-Lear, and McKellen's becoming-Lear in 2007 was different from his becoming-Lear in 2018. Similarly, working from my own philosophical text, my becoming-otherwise here and now will be different from other such becomings, including those that I have performed and those that I will perform in future.

One can make a pretense of playing Lear like Ian McKellen did in 2007 or in 2018 or like Glenda Jackson did in 2019, but one cannot make a pretense of performing my philosophy like anyone else; the role that I have written into being must be played "otherwise" or not at all. That being said, there are those who are ashamed of playing roles otherwise and there are those who shamelessly enjoy playing roles otherwise; I prefer the latter to the former, for the latter are remarkable in their differences while the former are unremarkable in spite of their differences: shamelessly different players baffle me, shamefully different players bore me.

Performance Notes:

3. Daring to Live

So few are disposed to believe that a philosophy may want to be more than the writings that are said to "contain" it, and that is because there are, indeed, so few philosophies today that want to be more than writings: most philosophers today write down certain truths so that they needn't dare to live, for to dare is to do without certain truths. It follows that, when I say that I am a philosopher, most assume that I am a man who writes down certain truths so that he needn't ever have to dare.

The surest proof that philosophers write so that they needn't dare to live is that they write long books and expect others to read them closely.

Borges' diagnosis of the writer's situation has always struck me as the most incisive one, "Writing long books is a laborious and impoverishing act of foolishness: expanding in five hundred pages an idea that could be perfectly explained in a few minutes. A better procedure is to pretend that those books already exist and to offer a summary, a commentary." All philosophers who write long books know, consciously or unconsciously, that Borges' diagnosis is the most magnificent rebuke of their way of life. If a given philosopher writes a lengthy book it is either because (i) that philosopher doesn't have the daring to live or (ii) that philosopher is paradoxically daring to live by writing. I find that the former is almost always the case: almost all philosophers who write volumes of truths are avoiding ever having to dare.

Performance Notes:

4. Making a Body Expressive

In *Building a Character*, Stanislavski speaks to me of "making the body expressive." To make Stanislavski's point clearer to myself, I speak to myself of "making the body active as opposed to reactive."

A terrestrial animal's body is reactive when its muscles must effectively fight gravity in order to maintain a balanced posture; or, in other words, a terrestrial animal's body is reactive when, in the process of losing its balance, the animal uses its muscles to regain its balance.

A terrestrial animal's body is active when its muscles are free to affect gravity because its skeleton is arrayed so as to maintain a balanced posture with the assistance of gravity; or, in other words, a terrestrial animal's body is active when, without ever losing its balance, the animal uses its muscles to shift its balance.

An active body is an expressive body, a body that expresses experiences; a reactive body is an oppressed body, a body forced to repress experiences. We express experiences with and through our bodies to the degree that we shift our balance without losing our balance. We are oppressed by the force of gravity and forced to repress experiences to the degree that we must use our muscles to fight gravity and recover from losses of balance.

If I aim to perform my philosophy, to use my body to express my philosophy, I must make my body as expressive as I possibly can, as active as I possibly can: I must learn to shift my balance in remarkable ways without ever losing my balance.

That being said, however, one cannot learn to shift one's balance in remarkable ways without risking one's balance, without taking chances that might result in a loss of balance. It follows that, in seeking to learning to shift one's balance in remarkable ways, one must affirm risking one's balance, chancing a loss of balance. That being said, however, to affirm risking one's balance is not to affirm losing one's balance: I risk losing my balance, yes, but the last thing I want is to lose my balance and I would be overjoyed if my fortunes were such that I never once lost my balance.

Performance Notes:

5. Spectators Unheeded

Another keen passage from Peter Brook's *The Empty Space*:

It is hard to understand the true notion of spectator, there and not there, ignored and yet needed. The [performer's] work is never for an audience, yet always is for one. The onlooker is a partner who must be forgotten and still constantly kept in mind: a [performance] is statement, expression, communication and a private manifestation of loneliness—it is always what Artaud calls a signal through the flames—yet this implies a sharing of experience, once contact is made.

Indeed. I cannot live according to my philosophy and simply leave it at that. I am compelled to perform for an audience, to make a life lived according to my philosophy something sensational, something spectacular. Yet, at the same time, I do not care not for any spectator's judgments regarding my performance, be they approving or disapproving judgments. Ay! It is the shameful performer who performs to receive the spectator's approving or disapproving judgments; the shameless performer performs so as to motivate the spectator to have done with judgment, to live and know otherwise.

Louis Aragon, recalling his aim in writing his tour de force *Le Paysan de Paris*, remarked, "I was seeking... a new kind of novel that would break all the traditional rules governing the writing of fiction... a novel that the critics would be obliged to approach empty-handed." To perform shamelessly is to perform with similar aims as these: a shameless performance is a performance that aims to both break with traditional rules and to baffle the critics' power of judgment. A shameless performance, when successful, motivates the spectator to have done with judgment and to live and know otherwise, at least for a moment but hopefully for a long time past the conclusion of the performance.

My performances shall dismiss audiences insofar as my performances shall say to them, "You can keep your judgment and shove it!"

My performances shall entreat audiences insofar as my performances shall say to them, "Have done with judgment! Come and (re)create otherwise alongside me!"

Performance Notes:

6. The Medium and the Message

To shift from being a philosopher-writer to being a philosopher-performer is to concern oneself less with parsing one's philosophical propositions and to concern oneself more with choreographing the gestures and enunciations that transmit one's philosophical propositions.

The philosopher-as-writer can pretend that the medium isn't the message, that their message is something apart from its transmission medium, but the philosopher-performer cannot pretend, the philosopher-as-performer has to know better: the medium is the message or, more precisely, the message is nothing apart from its transmission medium. This is not to say that a message can be reduced to its medium but, rather, that a message, although different from its medium, cannot be sensed or understood in any way whatsoever without reference to its medium: a message is something when considered along with its medium but nothing when considered apart from its medium. If one has a message of any profundity to transmit, one cannot switch one medium out for another medium without profoundly transforming the message that one transmits: only trivial messages will undergo trivial transformations when they are transmitted otherwise.

To express my philosophy with written words is one thing, to express my philosophy with life and limb is another. My philosophy, insofar as it isn't trivial, will undergo profound transformations as I endeavor to express it with life and limb in addition to expressing it with written words.

Performance Notes:

7. All the World is a Theatre

Most bodies can only assume a few different balanced postures: they tend to shift their balance in a few predictable ways so that they do not lose their balance: i.e., they only create minimally dispersed, non-uniform distributions of balanced postures.

Most minds can only assume a few different perspectives: i.e., they tend to shift their perspective in a few predictable ways so that they do not lose their perspective: they only create minimally dispersed, non-uniform distributions of perspectives.

When I perform my an-archism, when I live and know according to my philosophy, I challenge my body to create a maximally dispersed, uniform distribution of balanced postures without ever losing balance and I challenge my mind to create a maximally dispersed, uniform distribution of perspectives without ever losing perspective. That being said, however, I only challenge my body and mind in this way when I perform.

Life is not a series of performances but, rather, the production of a series of performances. Performing is the culminating phase of the production process, yes, but it is still only one phase of the production process, and it is only during this one phase that my body and mind are challenged to perform my anarchism and to live and know according to my philosophy. The other phases of the production process are preparations for the culminating phase, preparations for performances. I am not always performing, I am not always living and knowing according to my philosophy, yes, but when I am not performing, when I am not living and knowing according to my philosophy, I must be preparing to perform, I must be engaged in some preparatory phase of the production of a performance.

All the world is a theater, not just a stage. This theater has not one but countless stages and, what's more, it has costume and prop rooms, control booths, ateliers, scene shops, orchestra pits, catwalks, trap rooms, fly lofts, rehearsal spaces, administrative offices, meeting rooms, box offices, dressing rooms, green rooms, affiliated restaurants and kitchens, rooftop gardens, gift shops, libraries, lodgings, and countless other spaces that contribute in some way or other to the production of performances. More remarkably still, this theater is forever being renovated, new spaces are forever being added to existing spaces, and existing spaces that serve certain purposes are forever being converted to serve altogether different purposes.

www.ingramcontent.com/pod-product-compliance
Lightning Source LLC
Chambersburg PA
CBHW042000090426
42811CB00031B/1964/J